E.E. "DOC" SMITH

MORE WILDSIDE CLASSICS

Please see www.wildsidepress.com for a complete list!

E.E. "Doc" SMITH

by

JOE SANDERS

WILDSIDE PRESS

To James Mandleco

E.E. "Doc" SMITH

This edition published in 2006 by Wildside Press, LLC.
www.wildsidepress.com

E.E. "Doc" SMITH

Starmont Reader's Guide 24

JOE SANDERS

Series Editor: Roger C. Schlobin

Starmont House
Mercer Island, Washington
1986

Library of Congress Cataloging-in-Publication Data

Sanders, Joseph.
        E. E. "Doc" Smith

        Bibliography: p.
        Includes index
        1. Smith, E. E. (Edward Elmer), 1890-1965--Criticism
and interpretation. 2. Science fiction, American--
History and criticism. I   Title.
PS3537.M349Z87 1986   813'.52   85-30434
ISBN 0-916732-73-8
ISBN 0-916732-72-X (pbk.)

JOE SANDERS is Professor of English at Lakeland Community
College, Mentor, Ohio. He has written a large number of
book reviews, several essays (on subjects ranging from the
relation between science fiction and detective fiction to
the future of drugs in professional sports), and the book-
length Roger Zelazny: A Primary and Secondary Bibliography.
He currently is warping his children by enticing them to
read science fiction.

To James Mandleco

CONTENTS

Usually, the first edition of a book contains the most reliable text, especially when its publication was supervised by the writer. In Smith's case, that would mean the Fantasy Press editions of his major works, which are the texts referred to in the only previous book devoted to Smith, Ron Ellik and Bill Evans' encyclopedic The Universes of E. E. Smith (Chicago: Advent, 1966). However, Smith also kept close watch over the paperback editions of his novels, and he revised his first novel, The Skylark of Space, extensively for its first paperback edition. It also is true that the Fantasy Press editions are virtually unobtainable by most readers but that the paperback editions of Smith's major novels have remained unchanged in their printing by Pyramid, Jove, and now Berkley (even the Garland Press library reprints for some reason chose to use the paperback texts). I therefore have decided to use a double system of references; in each citation, the first page number refers to the first edition, while the second number refers to the paperback edition currently available as noted below.

CL   Children of the Lens. Reading, PA: Fantasy Press, 1954; New York: Pyramid, 1966.

FL   First Lensman. Reading, PA: Fantasy Press, 1950; New York: Pyramid, 1964.

GP   Galactic Patrol. Reading, PA: Fantasy Press, 1950; New York: Pyramid, 1964.

GL   Gray Lensman. Reading, PA: Fantasy Press, 1951; New York: Pyramid, 1965.

SSL   Second Stage Lensmen. Reading, PA: Fantasy Press, 1953; New York: Pyramid, 1965.

SDQ   Skylark DuQuesne. New York: Pyramid, 1966. This paperback is the first edition.

SS   The Skylark of Space. Providence, RI: Hadley Publishing Company, 1947; New York: Pyramid, 1958. Al Lewis' bibliography for Ellik and Evans' The Universes of E.E. Smith calls the Hadley edition the best hardcover edition; with some trepidation, I use it as the source of quotations, since this is the version of the novel that gained Smith's original reputation, not the much later revision.

SV   Skylark of Valeron. Reading, PA: Fantasy Press, 1949; New York: Pyramid, 1963.

ST   Skylark Three. Reading, PA: Fantasy Press, 1948; New
     York: Pyramid, 1963.
T   Triplanetary. Reading, PA: Fantasy Press, 1948; New
     York: Pyramid, 1965.

CHRONOLOGY OF LIFE AND WORKS

1890   May 2, Smith is born to Fred J. Smith and Caroline
        Mills Smith, Sheboygan, WI. Family moves to
        Spokane, WA.
1902   Family moves to Seneaquoteen, ID.
1914   June 7, Smith is graduated from the University of
        Idaho, Moscow, ID.
1915   Smith and Jeanne Craig MacDougall are married, Oc-
        tober 5. After a bull session with Carl D. Garby,
        Ph.D., Smith begins collaborating with Lee Hawkins
        Garby on a tale of spaceflight.
1916   Smith and Mrs. Garby complete about a third of
        their novel.
1917   Smith receives his M.S. in Chemistry from George
        Washington University, studying under Charles E.
        Munroe, whom Smith later considered "probably the
        greatest high-explosives man yet to live."
1918   Smith earns the Ph.D. in Chemistry, George Wash ing-
         gton University.
1919   Smith becomes Chief Chemist for F.W. Stock & Sons,
        Hillsdale, MI (until 1936), specializing in dough-
        nut mixes.
        Smith returns to the manuscript of The Skylark of
        Space; the novel is finished by early next year,
        when it begins making the rounds of potential
        publishers.
1922   Skylark is rejected by Bob Davis, editor of Argosy,
        with an encouraging personal letter.
1927   Seeing the April 1927 issue of Amazing Stories on
        the newsstands, Smith sends "Skylark" to editor T.
        O'Conor Sloane, who accepts it immediately. Smith
        splits the money with Mrs. Garby, and the novel is
        published as a collaboration.
1928   In August, The Skylark of Space begins as a three-
        part serial in Amazing Stories. Within a month,
        Sloane requests a sequel, and Smith begins work by
        himself.
1930   In August, Skylark Three begins as a three-part
        serial in Amazing Stories.
1931   Spacehounds of IPC begins in Amazing Stories in
        July.
1933   January issue of Astounding Stories announces

1934	_Triplanetary_ as forthcoming During winter into 1934, Smith works on _Skylark of Valeron_. Following collapse of _Astounding_'s publisher _Triplanetary_ is published as a four-part serial in _Amazing Stories_, beginning in the January issue. In June, a full-page editorial in the revived _Astounding Stories_ announces the forthcoming _Skylark of Valeron_, beginning in August; the novel is serialized in seven parts as a circulation-building ploy.
1936	In January, Smith begins a new job as Production Manager at Dawn Doughnut, Jackson, MI.
1937	_Galactic Patrol_ began serialization in _Astounding Stories_ (September–February 1938); first of the Lensmen series.
1939	October issue of _Astounding Science-Fiction_ begins serialization of _Gray Lensman_.
1940	Smith is guest of honor at the Second World Science Fiction Convention, Chicago, September 1-2; his speech is "What Does This Convention Mean?"
1941	A novelette, "The Vortex Blaster," appears in the last, July, issue of _Comet Stories_; first of the "Storm" Cloud series
1943	Smith is promoted to head of the Inspection Division at Kingsbury Ordinance Plant, LaPorte, IN.
1944	Smith is fired from job at Kingsbury for refusing to okay substandard shells.
1945	Smith returns to doughnut-mix business with J.W Allen, Chicago.
1946	The August issue of _Astounding Science-Fiction_ carries a notice of Thomas P. Hadley's book publication of _The Skylark of Space_; the limited edition of 1000 sells out by mail.
1947	The November issue of _Astounding Science-Fiction_ begins serialization of _Children of the Lens_. Fantasy Press publishes _Spacehounds of IPC_, first of the hardcover editions from this publisher that brought Smith's work to a new generation of readers.
1950	_First Lensman_ appears from Fantasy Press, never published in a magazine.
1953	March issue of Ray Palmer's _Other Worlds Science Stories_ publishes "Tedric," first story in what turns out to be a truncated series.
1957	Smith retires from his J W. Allen job.
1958	In May, a revised version of _The Skylark of Space_ is published in paperback by Pyramid, the first of the mass-market editions that reestablish Smith's popularity.

1959   A three-part serialization of The Galaxy Primes begins in the March issue of Amazing Science Fiction Stories.

1960   The July issue of Analog carries Smith's "Subspace Survivors," a novelette intended to begin a new series.
The Vortex Blaster is published, the last of Smith's books from Fantasy Press.

1961   If begins serialization of Masters of Space, Smith's posthumous collaboration with E. Everett Evans, in the November issue (concluded January 1962).

1963   On September 1, at 21st World Science Fiction Convention, Washington, D.C., Smith receives the First Fandom Hall-of-Fame Award; he announces Skylark DuQuesne as his next story.

1965   The July issue of IF begins a three-part serialization of Skylark DuQuesne.
August 31—Smith dies of a heart attack.
Subspace Explorers is published by Canaveral Press.

1975   The Best of E.E. 'Doc' Smith is published in England.

1976   Pyramid publishes Imperial Stars, an expansion of Smith's 1964 IF story, by Stephen Goldin; all future books in the Family d'Alembert series are by Goldin alone.

1978   Lord Tedric by Gordon Eklund is published, first of an abbreviated series tenuously inspired by Smith's work.

1982   Sixteenth printing of the Lensmen novels in paper back, by Berkley.

PREFACE

E.E. "Doc" Smith's novels are among the most widely and
persistently popular works of science fiction ever written.
Their appearances as magazine serials caused waves of
approval; their publication in hardcover by a specialty pub-
lisher won a new generation of fans. Eventually appearing
in paperback, they have been in print for over two decades.
Yet critics have never been comfortable with Smith's
writing. Especially in recent years, his work has been dis-
missed as "aesthetically and intellectually vacuous,"(1) and
he has been lumped with the primitive science-fiction hacks.
This is the first full-length study of his fiction.

I first encountered Smith's novels almost three decades
ago, as a high school student who discovered that a neighbor
was a longtime science-fiction fan who was willing to loan
books and magazines. Soon, seeing that I could be trusted
not to tear his property apart, Jim Mandleco loaned me his
most treasured books: Doc Smith's Skylark novels, then the
Lensmen series. I enjoyed them, then moved on through piles
of Golden Age Astoundings, etc., into college, teaching,
book reviewing, years of other activities. Much later, becoming aware of Smith's historical importance, I decided
that I should reread his novels. I was afraid to. Fairly
often, rereading books I enjoyed while young has shown
merely how limited I was as a young reader. In this case,
though, the reaction was much more complicated. I discovered that some things that had thrilled me the first time
through, such as the human characters in the Lensmen saga,
were rather sketchy. On the other hand, I discovered new
things that were very well done, including humor, sharp
observations, and skillful construction. And I discovered
more thought--and, yes, more wisdom--in Smith's novels than
I had been prepared to see earlier.

This study is intended to explain Smith's popularity
while countering some of the unthinking aversion Smith's
work has received. It provides a solid framework of factual
information, fleshed out with interpretations that are as
clearly supported and fair as possible. To be "fair" means
not ignoring the weaknesses of Smith's work but not ignoring
his strengths either. By and large, Smith manages to work
around the things he is unable or unwilling to handle in his
fiction. Rather than presupposing that any work of fiction
must do certain things, I have tried to understand why he

4

made such choices, and to estimate not only what those choices cost his work but what they permitted him to accomplish

I have had to make some choices, too. As in the case of all real choices, some valuable things have been slighted. This book concentrates on Smith's separate series, discussing each as a unified whole; since the writing of the different series sometimes overlapped or was interrupted by other projects, this approach does not quite manage to show the chronological development of Smith as a writer. Also, dealing with finished works, this book does not spend much space discussing how Smith revised his writing for book publication (except for some cursory comments on Second Stage Lensman) or how he revised different editions of The Skylark of Space. Nor does it have much time to explore exactly how Smith's writing influenced specific authors, such as John W. Campbell, Jr., or how Smith's work was itself influenced by the literary and social climate of his time. And finally, it cannot spend time on much personal description of Smith, who was one of the most beloved features at fan gatherings.

Basically, this book pursues several major themes, rather than risk getting lost in side avenues. Each chapter attempts to discuss a few major points related directly to Smith's writing, a choice that has necessitated including plot summaries near the beginning of each discussion. In critical writing, plot summaries are almost inevitably either so sketchy that they are worthless or so bloated that they overwhelm the critical commentary supposedly based on them. In either case, they take up space. Still, this especially galling choice had to be made. Delivering a conference paper later expanded into Chapter IV of this study, I was taken to task for summarizing too much; however, the lady who objected to any reference to plot mentioned that she had read the Lensmen series fifteen times and memorized large sections. For the sake of non-memorizers, recognizing that Smith's works tend to cluster in large and complex groups, I have grudgingly summarized as much as seemed necessary to prepare for the discussion that is the real goal.

I am thus aware how many interesting topics were squeezed out of this book and remain unexplored. The book's main point, however, is that there are interesting, serious things a reader can discover in Smith's writing. Discovering some has enriched my pleasure, and I hope others will make the effort, too.

The people who have given information and encouragement for this book include Jim Mandleco, Ben Jason, Al and Verna

5

Smith Trestrail, Mary T. Brizzi, Robert and Juanita Coulson, David A. Kyle, Howard DeVore, Forrest J Ackerman, William B. Ellern, Robert Reginald, Ray Beam, Lloyd Arthur Eshbach, Frederik Pohl, and Jack Williamson. My thanks also to Lakeland Community College for a sabbatical leave that helped me finish the actual writing.

NOTES

(1) Brian Stableford, "The Skylark Series," in Survey of Science Fiction Literature, Volume Five, ed. Frank N. Magill (Englewood Cliffs, NJ: Salem, 1979), p. 2094.

LIFE AND CAREER

Smith's life is worth some attention both because of the way he drew on experiences in his writing and because so many of the written reactions to his work are expressed in terms of admiration for Smith as a person.

Though Smith was born in Sheboygan, Wisconsin (May 2, 1890), his parents moved west that winter.(1) Smith's father had been a ship's carpenter and now turned his hand to carpentry work, eventually winding up farming on a homestead on the Pend d'Oreille River, in northern Idaho. Thus, to all intents and purposes, Smith was a young Westerner. Because of his family's reduced circumstances, Smith found himself basically on his own, in the sense of being responsible for and providing for himself, at a very early age. Besides the influence of personal circumstances, Smith grew up in a place and time that emphasized the kind of frontier personality now only dimly reflected in Western fiction. The ideal man, it seemed, was physically fit and was versatile in all manner of practical skills. His speech veered from laconic restraint to exaggeration and humorous boasting; even (or especially) the remarks showing intelligence or sensitivity were constructed out of humorous slang, and he became less articulate the more emotionally stirred he was. He was always ready to join with others to protect women, children, or the less strong, but he himself had to respond to challenges alone, without waiting for help. This ideal Western man shows up many times in Smith's work, especially as Richard Seaton in the Skylark series and as Steve Stevens in Spacehounds of IPC. First, though, he was Smith himself.

That was a difficult ideal for a twelve-year-old boy to live up to. Sometimes it was physically dangerous as well. Smith later told his children of the night, when he was the youngest log boss in an Idaho lumber camp, that the envious camp cook got drunk on a mixture of vanilla and lemon extract and chased "Kid Smith" up a tree, where he remained trapped until morning. But Smith stuck out the difficult jobs, gathering the fund of practical experience that would later convince readers like Robert A. Heinlein that a man shipwrecked on an alien world could have expertise in enough fields to rebuild the technology to rescue himself, an event in Spacehounds of IPC.

At about the same time, Smith's gentle, intelligent

mother, a former schoolteacher, encouraged the boy to get an education, and he attended the college prep school for the University of Idaho, starting in the tenth grade. Smith had left home after a quarrel with his father; it was with financial support from his sisters and brothers that he enrolled in the University of Idaho. He loved it. For a talented high achiever, the University offered a smorgasbord of things in which to achieve. Smith had a straight A record, majoring in Chemical Engineering and winning a scholarship in his junior year for scholastic excellence. In addition, he was captain of the rifle team and took part in other sports (somewhat hampered by injuries he had suffered a few years earlier, when he jumped from the fourth floor of a burning building), sang bass lead in the Gilbert and Sullivan operettas, and was president of the chemistry club, the chess club, and the guitar and mandolin club. He also turned an interest in photography into income by taking pictures for the school and the local newspaper to pay part of his college expenses. And he was absorbing other things as well, as shown by the names of some classmates that show up in his fiction, such as Virgil Samms, hero of First Lensman.

One day in his senior year, Smith noticed a photo of a beautiful girl on the desk of his roommate, Allan MacDougall. When Smith regretfully remarked that it was too bad she was already spoken for or he'd be interested in her, MacDougall replied, "Oh, you can have her. That's just my sister." After Smith and Jeanne MacDougall had corresponded for a time, they met and almost immediately became engaged. Smith moved to Washington, D.C., after graduating from the University in 1914, having taken a job as chemist at the Bureau of Standards. He and Jeanne were married on October 5, 1915.

Also in 1915, an unexpectedly momentous event took place. Smith had become friends with Carl and Lee Hawkins Garby, a young couple who were his next-door neighbors in the Seaton Place Apartments. One hot, stuffy night the two couples were idly visiting when Carl Garby remarked that he wished they were in outer space where it was so much cooler. As the subject caught the group's attention and the conversation became livelier, it developed that Garby was echoing comments Smith had made several days before at a chemists' smoker. Mrs. Garby suggested that Smith write a story that would present his ideas on outer space. At first, Smith demurred. He might be able to handle the main plotting (certainly that first novel shows imaginative fluency, especially a willingness to let actions emerge naturally out of a sharply visualized situation). However, Smith protested that he couldn't do the characters (in particular, the love element of popular fiction was a very formalized, tricky area). When Mrs. Garby replied that if he'd handle the rest of it she would do the love interest, Smith was intrigued enough to actually sit down with her and begin work on The Skylark of Space. The two did an outline; then one would write a chapter and give it to the other for criticism, then re-revise it, and so on. By the end of 1916, they had completed about one-third of the story. In addition to the love interest, Mrs. Garby contributed ideas such as Crane's music room and the Osnomian banquet hall; meanwhile, reading and correcting all aspects of the manuscript, Smith developed more confidence in his ability to handle characters. For protagonists, the writers essentially transposed the Smiths into the Seatons and the Garbys into the Cranes; Smith and Garby's tennis games, Smith's fondness for motorcycles, etc., were simply moved as a whole into the novel.

With the novel unfinished, Smith left Washington in 1918 to become an organic chemist for F.W. Stock & Sons, Hillsdale, MI, specializing in doughnut mixes, a position he was to hold until 1936. The following year, his thoughts again turned to the "Skylark," and he took up the manuscript again, completing it himself.(2) Smith submitted the finished manuscript to book publishers and to several magazines that published science fiction along with other adventure fiction, but it proved too advanced for any established market; in particular, Bob Davis, editor of Argosy, sent Smith a personal letter praising the story but regretfully explaining that his readership would not be able to follow it. Finally, in 1927, Smith saw an issue of Hugo Gernsback's Amazing Stories and sent the manuscript off once again. The novel's enthusiastic reception, partially described and explained in the next chapter, inspired Smith to begin work on a sequel to "Skylark."

It is important to remember, however, that Smith was not a full-time writer. For one thing, he could not afford to be. He received $125 from Amazing for The Skylark of Space; when he split this sum with Mrs. Garby, he was left with less than he had spent in postage during the years he had submitted the manuscript to many publishers. Even though his word rates increased after that, since he was the biggest name in science fiction, he could never have supported himself and his family by writing. Rather, Smith seems to have treated science fiction as one element in a well-rounded life. He worked at his profession. He kept up his athletic activities and developed new ones; he was Michigan Amateur Open Golf Champion at the Hillsdale Country

9

Club, rode in motorcycle meets, and practiced archery until he became a senior Boy Scout advisor for merit badges. He also spent time with his family. Smith and his wife gave a lot of attention to their three children, Verna, Clarissa, and Roderick. They took the children everywhere, did everything with them. Smith shared his interest in athletics and music, and he read the short stories of Jack London and Sir Arthur Conan Doyle to his brood. Looking back, Verna suspects that her parents were building an ideal life for their children to compensate for the rough life they had led themselves. Meanwhile, Smith observed his bright, competitive children and absorbed the behaviors he would later depict in Children of the Lens.

One major difference that writing did make in Smith's life was his discovery of science-fiction fandom and vice versa. Smith's exchanges with other correspondents in the letter column of Amazing, following the publication of his early novels, show his delight in trading ideas and shooting the breeze in general. As readers begin to write to each other directly and to publish amateur magazines and seek each other out in person, they naturally contacted Smith and he just as naturally supplied material for several fanzines.(3) He got along well with fans in person, too. As Guest of Honor at the Second World Science Fiction Convention, during Labor Day weekend in Chicago, 1940, Smith delivered a forceful pro-fandom speech entitled "What Does This Convention Mean?" He also attended the convention's masquerade in his leather motorcycle uniform, carrying a homemade raygun, as a character from C. L. Moore's fiction, Northwest Smith. It was also at the convention that Smith met several fans who lived near him, such as John Millard from Jackson and E. E. Evans from Battle Creek. In spring of 1941, a group began meeting twice a month at Smith's home to discuss science fiction and especially to preview whatever manuscript Smith was working on at the time. Smith kept contact with this group, The Galactic Roamers, and acknowledged their helpful suggestions to his work in an afterword to Second Stage Lensmen. He was also a regular attendee at conventions after that, becoming legendary for the amount of direct attention he was willing to pay to individual fans, however young or old, famous or unknown they might be. Researching Smith's life, I have repeatedly heard him described as "a real human being," "a personal friend," "the finest man I've ever met," or simply as "good." Much as these remarks sound like stale cliches, Smith evidently had the rare sincerity required to bring them to life.

Meanwhile, his growth as a science-fiction writer continued. In the 1930s, Smith began his major science-fiction work. After writing two novels that seemed at the time to be false starts because they did not lead to series, Smith planned an immense, 400,000 work novel in four sections--the Lensmen novels. He prepared a detailed summary of the story and even wrote and polished the climax of "Children of the Lens" very early in the process. Then, in a sustained siege of creative energy, he produced the first three novels at a rate of about one every other year, "Galactic Patrol" beginning serialization in the fall of 1937. The complete Lensmen saga is discussed in Chapter V of this study.

Despite the personal satisfactions Smith was discovering, his career was rather turbulent at the time. In 1936, he shifted jobs, moving to Dawn Doughnut in Jackson, MI. With the coming of World War II, that job evaporated. Smith tried his hand at writing non-science-fiction stories, dealing with a nurse, a motorcycle policeman, etc. He also worked on "Trestrail," an autobiographical novel.(4) During the first part of the war, Smith worked at the Kingsbury Ordinance Plant, in a special laboratory called "Outer Siberia" because it was located far away from the other buildings in case of explosion. Smith became increasingly disillusioned with the management's emphasis on production quantity rather than quality, and he finally was fired in 1944 for refusing to okay what he believed to be substandard shells. He described this episode in "1941," one of the new chapters he wrote to tie the stray novel Triplanetary into the Lensmen series. After that, Smith worked at Allis Chalmers, [West Allis, WI] first on the assembly line, later in charge of their heat treatment division. Finally, in 1945, he was able to return to the doughnut mix business with a baking supply company, J. W. Allen of Chicago, a position he kept until he retired in 1957.

With this new security, Smith returned to science-fiction writing, finishing "Children of the Lens." He also became involved in the hardcover publication of his novels. At the time, strange as it may seem, though Smith was a famous and respected writer within the science-fiction field, his novels had never appeared in book form. They were available only as installments of serials within the magazines.(5) It must have been very satisfying for Smith when Thomas Hadley approached him and proposed publishing The Skylark of Space in book form. True, Hadley was so inexperienced in merchandising the book that no one knew it existed for awhile, but a brief mention in the August 1946 Astounding led to the 1,000-copy printing being sold out by mail within a month. Lloyd A. Eshbach, who had stepped in

11

to help Hadley promote the book, then formed Fantasy Press to publish outstanding magazine science fiction in hardcover editions; the first author he contacted was Smith, since he had Hadley's mailing list and knew he could sell at least 1,000 copies of a Smith novel. From 1947 (Spacehounds of IPC) to 1960 (The Vortex Blaster), Fantasy Press published all of Smith's available novels, including one novel that never appeared in a magazine at all, First Lensman. The royalties were never large—not much more than $1,000 or so per book—but those editions not only satisfied Smith's older fans but brought Smith to the attention of a new generation of readers. And Smith quite evidently took the Fantasy Press editions very seriously, devoting considerable attention to polishing the novels for book publication.

While Smith was finishing his long-term Lensmen project and revising his novels for book publication, science-fiction was undergoing considerable growth and change. Smith had trouble fitting in. Following retirement in 1957, he was eager to take on new projects. Yet it was not until 1960 that John W. Campbell, Jr., published "Subspace Survivors" (Analog, July)—the last story of Smith's that he ever accepted. Meanwhile, very little new work appeared from Smith in the late 1950s, with the exception of a thorough revision of The Skylark of Space for paperback publication (especially by abridging the opening sections that still reflected Smith's initial uncertainty about how far he could stretch the conventions of popular fiction) and the novel The Galaxy Primes that Amazing printed in 1959 but in a severely edited version that displeased Smith. Since this novel obviously had been written to appeal to Campbell, Analog's rejection of it must have been especially galling.(6) As usual, though, when confronted with a problem, Smith worked his way through it. He found a more sympathetic editor in Frederik Pohl, editor of Galaxy and IF. Pohl had admired Smith's works for years, and he was willing to work patiently editing stories written in the style of Smith's later years, one that reduced the amount of connected narrative and relied more on separate, sometimes cryptic, scenes. Smith accepted Pohl's fleshing out of his stories in relatively good grace. He simply continued working as he always had, doing the very best he could.

He kept busy. Smith's last years were spent in giving a parting touch to the Skylark series, Skylark DuQuesne, and in optimistically beginning two new series, with Subspace Explorers (a novel based on his last story in Analog) and with "Imperial Stars" in IF, beginning the Family d'Alembert series that was continued by Stephen Goldin.

A major event in Smith's life was his winning the First

Fandom Hall-of-Fame Award at the 21st World Science Fiction Convention, Washington, D.C., in recognition of his contributions to the genre; it was a very emotional ceremony, the only time Smith was ever at a loss for words in public. Two years later, while Skylark DuQuesne was appearing in IF, Smith and his wife went to visit her sister on the west coast. They went out to dinner in Portland on August 31, and later that night, after a brief surge of pain, Smith was dead of a heart attack. His meticulously maintained files and notes were first shipped from his retirement home in Florida to his wife's new dwelling, with her sister. After Mrs. Smith's death a few years later, they were sent to his daughter Verna Smith Trestrail, in northern Indiana, where they still await cataloging and study. Already, they have yielded the sequel to Subspace Explorers, edited for publication by Lloyd A. Eshbach, and a detective novel, Have Trench Coat--Will Travel, that Smith worked on after retirement and that soon may be published.

Whatever else turns up, however, Smith already has earned a place in science-fiction history. His reputation lives on. In 1966, the Lensmen series was one of five nominated for a special Hugo Award as "Best All-Time Series." An annual science-fiction convention in Moscow, Idaho, home of the University of Idaho, honors Smith's work. He is referred to in the new chemical tables published by Omni, May 1981. And, most impressive of all, his books have reached an entirely new audience in paperback editions. His work is still in print, currently in 25 languages. Obviously Smith is a major voice in science-fiction.

The people who knew Smith have no doubt of his significance. Robert A. Heinlein's memoir is an enthusiastic tribute to Smith's versatility and integrity. Frederik Pohl, in an editorial entitled "Edward E. Smith, Ph.D.," (IF, December 1965), comments that "Smith's characters used technology as a tool. Science didn't scare them. They were on top of it at every step." In a recent letter, Pohl adds that Smith "opened the universe for readers and writers in a way no one else had done."(7) And Jack Williamson--who hitchhiked from New Mexico years ago to visit Smith-- mentions earlier writers on interstellar themes but adds that

> Doc Smith hits us harder. His Skylark of Space touched off an explosion in many young imaginations, including my own . . . I was vastly excited by the wider light-years it opened to my own young visions of interstellar adventure . . . Doc did as much as anybody to

create the optimistic dream of a triumphant
human interstellar future, the dream I like to
call the basic myth of modern science-fiction.
Done a bit more slickly than Doc ever did it,
that myth still animates a lot of current space
operas—often written by people who shrink from
calling them that. It's even the backbone of
nearly all the great space adventures that have
lately been capturing so many millions in the
tube and on the screen.(8)

The descriptions of Smith as a person and as a writer
fit together neatly; his admirers see him as an impressive
man who produced impressive works. Somehow, Smith managed
to get his own confidence and determination into his
fiction. The following chapters will discuss in more detail
how he accomplished this and what rewards his writing has
for readers today.

NOTES

(1) Facts in this discussion of Smith's life are drawn
from the chapter on Smith in Sam Moskowitz, Seekers of
Tomorrow: Masters of Modern Science Fiction
(Cleveland: World, 1965); Redd Boggs, "Flight of the
Skylarks," Spaceship #25 (June 1954); Robert A.
Heinlein, "Larger Than Life: A Memoir in Tribute to
Dr. Elmer E. Smith," in Expanded Universe: The New
Worlds of Robert A. Heinlein (New York: Grosset,
1980); a taped interview session conducted by Howard
DeVore, 28 June 1980, for the SF Oral History
Association; an autobiographical sketch by Smith him-
self in Other Worlds Science Stories, March 1953;
Lloyd Arthur Eshbach's Over My Shoulder: Reflections
on a Science Fiction Era (Philadelphia: Train, 1983);
and on correspondence and interviews with Albert and
Verna Smith Trestrail, Frederik Pohl, and Jack
Williamson. Sources of individual bits of fact are
cited only occasionally during the chapter; divergent
accounts are noted only when they might seriously af-
fect interpretations.

(2) Accounts differ on this point. According to
Moskowitz, Smith simply did the remainder of the writing by himself, informing Garby of his progress; Boggs
quotes Smith as saying he and Garby collaborated by
mail, sending chapters back and forth as they had
handed them back and forth earlier; in the taped
interview, Smith's daughter Verna recalls that the

14

original manuscript was lost in the interval between its completion and the submission to Amazing, so that the entire published work was Smith's from beginning to end. In any event, though Lee Hawkins Garby's name was listed as a collaborator in the first appearances of The Skylark of Space, Smith was responsible for the finished work.

(3) Tantalizing references are to be found in Sam Moskowitz's The Immortal Storm: A History of Science Fiction Fandom (Atlanta: ASFO Press, 1954). The material itself, given the small circulation and rapid disappearance of most fanzines, is virtually impossible to locate or examine.

(4) None of these works has been published, and the novel apparently was never finished. Its title, incidentally, is the name of Smith's son-in-law, Al, for Smith felt his own name was too bland.

(5) It must be said, however, that back issues of the magazines were widely available for purchase or exchange from many fans, and many could still be located in used book stores. Thus, Smith's fame had continued among some newer readers.

(6) Overall, Smith's love-hate relationship with Campbell would rate a lengthy study itself, from their respectful but determined debates in the letter column of Amazing (when Smith was an established writer and Campbell was barely beginning to write stories that could rival Smith's superscientific space operas) to the sometimes testy private correspondence of their later years (when Smith was a writer submitting manuscripts to meet Campbell's editorial demands). It should be noted that Campbell showed real kindness to Smith, as in an unexpected letter of 11 June 1947, in which he passed on word that a science-fiction reader in the Navy had inspired the method of coordinating information used in the Lensmen novels to develop the system that the U.S. used to defeat the Japanese in the Pacific. It also should be noted that in later years Campbell derided Smith's writing as primitive and that he only reluctantly published Children of the Lens.

(7) Letter of 15 September 1982.

(8) Letter of 17 September 1982.

IV

THE SKYLARK SAGA

The editor's blurb for the first installment of The
Skylark of Space is striking in its mixture of habitual
decorum with a recognition that something phenomenal is at
hand:

> Perhaps it is a bit unethical and unusual for
> editors to voice their opinions of their own
> wares, but when such a story as The Skylark of
> Space comes along, we just feel as if we must
> shout from the housetops that this is the
> greatest interplanetarian and space flying story
> that has appeared this year. Indeed, it prob-
> ably will rank as one of the great space flying
> stories for many years to come.(1)

Readers agreed. In the issue that published the third, concluding installment of the novel, the editor mentions that
he already has received a flood of letters. "Discussions,"
Amazing's letter column, also shows what an impact Smith's
story had on readers.
    Before analyzing the reasons for the Skylark novels'
success, however, let us see what happens in each book.
Part of their success, after all, is due to their being interesting stories.
    Roughly the first third of The Skylark of Space
(condensed slightly by Amazing to make up the first installment of the serial, (2) takes place on Tellus, (Smith's
favorite term for Earth), but it is full of action. After
discovering how to release interatomic energy, by stumbling
on the rare metal "X"'s reaction with copper, Richard Seaton
resigns his job as chemist for a government bureau and forms
a partnership with his friend, millionaire Martin Crane, to
experiment with and develop X as a source of electrical
power and as the propulsion for a spaceship. Unfortunately,
they are detected by Seaton's workmate, Marc "Blackie"
DuQuesne, who is almost Seaton's physical and mental equal
but who is as unscrupulous as Seaton is virtuous. DuQuesne
allies himself with the criminal businessmen of World Steel
and plans to steal Seaton's work. As both sides build
spaceships, DuQuesne and a criminal accomplice kidnap
Dorothy Vaneman, Seaton's fiancee, planning to trade her for
the secret. During a struggle between the gangster and Mar-

garet Spencer, another victim of World Steel, DuQuesne's spaceship is shot off into the far reaches of space, where it drifts helplessly into the gravity field of a dead star. Crane and Seaton follow in their spaceship, The Skylark of Space, and rescue DuQuesne and the two girls. Their own supply of copper fuel used up by the escape from the dead star, they must find a planet where they can obtain a fresh store of copper. They first visit a world where life struggles at the Carboniferous level (but on which they discover a rich lode of X), then a world on which a disembodied intelligence menaces them by its ability to materialize in different forms and by its threat to dematerialize them. Finally, they discover a cluster of green suns rich in copper and arrive on the planet Osnome just as an immense monster is about to devour an airship. They save the humans aboard the ship and are apparently welcomed as honored guests by the nation of Mardonale. Seaton and his party are approached, however, by slaves who give them almost instantaneous instruction via a learning-machine, showing that the Mardonalians actually plan to murder them. Therefore, Seaton and the others travel to Mardonale's rival nation, Kondal, where the two couples (Crane and Margaret have fallen in love, too) are married and where Seaton and Crane share their knowledge with the Kondalians and repulse an invasion by Mardonale. Once the Skylark is rebuilt of superhard Osnomian metal and fueled with plenty of copper, the Tellurians return home, where DuQuesne, who has cooperated with the others during the voyage, is allowed to escape.

Skylark Three, serialized in Amazing Stories (August-October 1930), begins with DuQuesne again scheming with World Steel to overcome Seaton; however, he leaves Tellus almost immediately on a mysterious voyage. Almost simultaneously, Seaton, Crane, and their wives are visited by the Osnomian nobleman they rescued from slavery in Mardonale; another planet in the Green System has attacked Osnome, and the Osnomians request aid. While the two Tellurian couples are on their way in Skylark Two, however, they are attacked by a superior alien spaceship that they manage to defeat only by means of an experimental device that Seaton had been playing around with--a zone of force impervious to energy and matter. The attacking ship was an advance scout for the Fenachrone, a humanoid race that considers itself bound to rule the universe by wiping out any inferiors; the ship had sent a warning message home before Seaton destroyed it, and a Fenachrone fleet will be launched against Tellus and Osnome soon. Armed with this new threat, Seaton convinces the two warring planets of the Green System to unite to save themselves. He realizes, however, that he

17

needs more knowledge to fight the Fenachrone, so he begins to tour the system to locate an older civilization that can help him. Simultaneously, DuQuesne, who had found traces of Fenachrone exploration during his earlier trip, rescues a survivor from the ship Seaton destroyed and begins the journey back to the Fenachrone system. Meanwhile, Seaton visits the planet Dasor and meets its porpoise people, then finds the vastly advanced civilization he seeks on the planet Norlamin. The Norlaminians share many wonders with Seaton and his companions, especially the ability to project themselves physically over vast distances, using a variation of the instant educational machine encountered in the first novel. Using the immense knowledge thus obtained, Seaton creates the vastly improved spaceship Skylark Three and destroys the Fenachrone space fleet, then the planet itself, finally an escaping ship intended to found another colony of the malevolent race. DuQuesne and his accomplice apparently were incinerated when their ship approached the Fenachrone system.

The first order of business in "Skylark of Valeron," serialized in Astounding Stories in seven parts as a circulation builder (August 1934 to February 1935) is to resurrect DuQuesne. It turns out that DuQuesne had constructed animated dummies to draw the Fenachrone fire; then, after the decoys were burned to ash, DuQuesne and his accomplice hijacked a Fenachrone warship. Now they travel back to Norlamin to lie their way to a share of the advanced knowledge that Seaton was given. Seaton and his party, meanwhile encounter a cluster of the disembodied intelligences that threatened them in the first novel; to escape, they rotate the smaller Skylark Two into the fourth dimension, where they encounter and fight their way through incomprehensible beings and lands. When they return to normal space, however, they find that they have traveled so far that they have no idea how to find their familiar sector of space. They soon stumble into a solar system in which the Chlorans, a race of chlorine-breathing ameboids, are menacing a human race on the planet Valeron, and they use their accumulated knowledge and power to save the humans and send the ameboids' planet to another star where they will not trouble anyone. With the resources of their new allies, they build a vast new spaceship to house a computer capable of mapping their surroundings. Discovering familiar stars, the two couples sail for home in The Skylark of Valeron. In the meantime, DuQuesne has returned to Tellus and seized control with the Fenachronian and Norlaminian science he has acquired. On the voyage home, however, Seaton traps the immortal pure intelligences, and when he gets back to Tellus he disembodies DuQuesne and imprisons his rival's cold intelligence with the others, sending the lot on a voyage through intergalactic space and various dimensions that should keep them out of mischief for an almost infinite period.

Skylark DuQuesne, serialized in Worlds of IF Science Fiction (June to October 1965), refers back to many elements of the earlier novels; its plot is extremely difficult to summarize, especially since so many things happen simultaneously. The action begins when Seaton's satisfaction is shattered by a Norlaminian announcement that the disembodied intelligences will soon be freed; the others may not return, but DuQuesne certainly will come back for vengeance. Rather than wandering through space looking for someone who has special knowledge that will help them overcome this new threat, Seaton and his cohorts broadcast a telepathic alert call. One group interested by the guarded message is the Jelmi, a race of humans enslaved by the monstrous, utterly logical and emotionless Llurdi; when a group of Jelmi revolt, the Llurdi set them "free," confident they can recapture them at any time but that the humans will produce useful inventions in the meantime. The Jelmi set up a secret base on Tellus' moon, where they cautiously study mankind. Meanwhile, DuQuesne has been returned to physical form by the disembodied intelligences, who find him unworthy to accompany them in their wanderings because of his raging emotions. He sets course for Tellus, but on the way encounters a Llurdi ship and realizes that these aliens are not only a threat to humanity in general but have him outgunned. Accordingly, he contacts Seaton and makes an alliance of necessity—though he sends Seaton off on a wild goose chase in the wrong direction. In fact, though, while DuQuesne meets the Jelmi and obtains a fourth-dimensional transportation device they have just discovered, Seaton runs into a scout from a Chloran-ruled galaxy that damages The Skylark of Valeron severely, so that Seaton and his friends decide to lie low and spy out information on the Chlorans. After organizing a coup on one of the human slave-worlds of the Chlorans, the crew of the Skylark returns to familiar territory, figuring out DuQuesne's ruse in the meantime. Simultaneously, the Jelmi use their fourth-dimensional transporter to threaten the Llurdi and convince those logical beings not to interfere with their freedom, and DuQuesne rescues the last survivors of the Fenachrone, who had been picked up by the Llurdi and subjected to scientific observation ever since; he uses them to crew his immense, overwhelmingly-armed version of the Skylark. The Skylark of Valeron, meanwhile, approaches the Llurdi main planet and

19

engages in a test of strength before the Jelmi intervene and show that there is no need for conflict. With that threat out of the way, Seaton is free to respond to another call from DuQuesne, who has just discovered the Chloran menace and again realizes he needs help. The two antagonists come together with a wide variety of people possessing psychic power—in particular, "witches" from the planet Seaton liberated from the Chlorans—and form a psychic unit that explodes the suns of the Chloran planets throughout that galaxy, while transferring the slave-planets safely to another galaxy. This done, characters return to their respective homes, while DuQuesne and a beautiful, strong-minded woman he has long admired head out on their own to found an empire.

Obviously, the Skylark novels increased dramatically in complexity and scope over the years. The series has been, by several measures, one of the most dynamic and creative in the history of science fiction. Yet its writing was interrupted several times by other projects, and Smith tried at least twice to put the capstone on the series and walk away from it. The reasons for this apparent contradiction have to do with the basis of the series' success, and that has to do with the immediate and lasting appeal of The Skylark of Space and its sequel.

Why was the first Skylark such a sweeping success? Looking back from over half a century later, it is difficult to see exactly what the novel accomplished. it might be easy to assume, looking at the reprints by Wells, Verne, Poe, etc., that occupied the early issues of Amazing Stories, that Smith was simply the first of the contemporary American writers who could do publishable work. That would be misleading. Thanks to the efforts of H. Bruce Franklin, Sam Moskowitz, and others, we are becoming aware of the huge amount of science fiction published in general magazines around the turn of the century—until, in fact, it became largely restricted in America to specialized magazines like Amazing Stories. Whatever his rank among the early science-fiction writers, Smith was not the earliest.

Somewhat more plausibly, some argue that Smith's work succeeded because of his imagination; other writers at the time were more inhibited, straining over the details of inventions to make them seem plausible rather than employing them freely. There is truth in this; certainly one can think of early stories that spend their time laboring to prepare for a trip to the Moon—while one happens offstage, as a preliminary test, in the tenth chapter of The Skylark of Space. However, this is an oversimplification, too. Consider Edmond Hamilton's "Crashing Suns," a two-part serial

20

that began in Weird Tales (August 1928) the same month as
the first installment of Smith's novel.(3)   In that story,
the League of Planets sends a space ship out to investigate
a star rushing toward Earth's sun. the commander of the Interplanetary Patrol discovers that monstrous natives of the
rogue sun's planets intend to drive the two stars together
to generate heat to sustain their race. He escapes home and
returns with a battlefleet of space ships, winning at the
last instant when a human scientist duplicates the device
the enemy uses to control their sun and thus splits the star
apart.   There certainly is nothing timid about Hamilton's
scope. Or, looking even farther back into the hoard of
science-fiction stories in general magazines, consider "The
Planet Juggler" by J. George Frederick, in the November 1908
issue of All-Story Magazine. In that tale, Earth is held
for ransom by Canopus, a mysterious being from outer space
who broadcasts threats to throw the Earth into the sun. Led
by the great scientist Elverson, humanity decides to fight
back.   Elverson discovers how to control the Earth's move-
ment himself and steers it through space (along the way
picking up Mars and a star also threatened by Canopus) to a
showdown with Canopus. In all, it is clear that however
well Smith used his imagination he was not the first to imagine interstellar flight, planets and suns tossed about,
etc.

     However, it is not true that Smith was only doing bet-
ter the things that others already were doing. He contributed something very important to science fiction.   In
his work, from The Skylark of Space on, Smith created a
sense of scientific thinking taking place. From that accomplishment comes the basic interest of the Skylark novels;
it also raises some important considerations considering
Smith's employment of the imagination in writing his fiction
and in particular his building characters.

     We forget, looking back, how uneasily early science
fiction regarded science. If science had the power to
transform the world, it could be viewed as black magic as
easily as white. The scientist could be seen as a wizard,
pursuing his arcane studies in secret and appearing suddenly
to reveal--what? Taking Mary Shelley's Frankenstein as a
fantasy bordering on science fiction or, as Brian Aldiss
prefers, the first science-fiction novel, a reader notes
that the scientist Frankenstein and the explorer Walton (in
the book's framing story) both dream of accomplishing great
things for humanity but that they both attempt to do so by
isolating themselves from humanity. In their isolation,
they both are led to take actions that could destroy themselves and other humans. Frankenstein goes too far and is

lost; Walton, to whom Frankenstein tells his story, has time to turn back and be saved. A similar pattern occurs in much early science fiction. Even in the work of H. G. Wells, the scientist himself seldom speaks to the reader directly; his experience is almost always framed, distanced by an observer-commentator who can soften and question the scientist's assertions of physical accomplishment and ethical purity.

In much early science fiction, thus, despite its apparent praise of the scientist and his accomplishments, the real attitude was rather equivocal. Or even if the scientist was admired, he worked offstage, appearing suddenly to dazzle an audience with the fruits of his genius. In Frederick's "The Planet Juggler," for example, Elverson deduces that Canopus must be "some hermit scientist who is using his power rapaciously,"(4) and authorities on the distant planet later confirm that Canopus "'was once a foremost scientist and astronomer here . . . . He is greatly feared by his employees, because of his wizard-like power and his control over destructive forces'" (p. 533). Even Elverson, the genius who saves humanity, exhibits some of the same traits. While he is waiting for Canopus' messages, Elverson's "eyes glowed supernaturally in the violet tube-light over the desk" (p. 511); when he retreats to his laboratory to produce scientific marvels to defeat Canopus, he becomes "an object of mystery" himself (p. 517); and he can speak as "imperiously" as Canopus when dealing with lesser minds (p. 526). In similar fashion, Hamilton's "Crashing Suns" shows the scientist Sarto San retreating to his laboratory while Earth's fleet attacks the approaching menace. The other humans are astonished when Sarto San produces his miraculous invention at the last moment.

In these not atypical stories, a scientist is somehow apart from the reader. Even when he is beneficent, there is a hint of mystery, possibly menace, about him. Certainly, the reader is not encouraged to imagine sharing the kind of thinking or understanding that are a scientist's. This is a curious situation, for science fiction is based on the notion that humanity can understand and possibly control the whole of human experience. Some stories test and qualify this idea, and some wind up distinctly unhappy with the results; it still exists as the distinctive quality of science fiction. Yet early writers and presumably readers had a difficult time approaching the scientist as a representative of humanity, uncertain about sharing not merely the use of a particular device but also the kind of thinking that produced the device.

Smith's work is different. He manages to show the excitement of using a device because he manages to convey the excitement of _thinking_ the device into being. In a somewhat defensive introduction to an edition of Hamilton's Outside the Universe, another wild space opera first published in Weird Tales (July-October 1929), Donald A. Wollheim states that

> Edmond Hamilton didn't stop to explain how his ships worked, how their defenses operated, how they countered the problems of space-time, of light years, of space-ship ecology—he didn't have to . . . . The purpose of the novel was not an exposition of advanced mechanics; it was an entertainment of starry voyaging, a thrill-a-page yarn to tickle the reader's sense of wonder and that was all.(5)

Much of the description could fit Smith's work, too. But Smith's "advanced mechanics" still _feel_ plausible, because readers witness Seaton developing them. His first, fumbling tests of X lay vital groundwork for his later intergalactic voyages. Readers can observe the stages of Seaton's developing understanding, symbolized in the physical trans-formation of the series of Skylarks themselves.

The quality that makes Smith's fiction uniquely strik-ing is his depiction of the process of scientific thinking as the very heart of his story. And what makes this process especially dramatic and exciting is that it very soon be-comes a shared experience—the heart of a life-and-death duel that essentially serves to emphasize the importance of clear thinking.

At the beginning of The Skylark of Space, Richard Seaton is exposed to a startling event. He must make sense of it, despite the jeers of uncomprehending, uninterested people around him. (One of the roots of scientific thinking is the ability to recognize something out of the ordinary when it happens.) When Seaton begins exchanging ideas with Crane, this refining of thought as the two stimulate each other creates a dramatic sense of intelligence at work. And with the appearance of Blackie DuQuesne, the sense of wit-nessing deft scientific experimentation in action becomes even more vital. Scientific thought involves reaching for reliable principles, testing hypotheses. What Seaton and DuQuesne do for each other is even more interesting than what they do to each other. They press each other mercilessly, making each other strain to find the weakness in a working hypothesis, race ahead to the next level of understanding, and stand poised there for the next extension of effort, never complacent, never satisfied with partial understanding and control.

I believe this was one of the major factors that made The Skylark of Space so freshly exciting when it first appeared. I believe it accounts for much of the novel's continuing appeal: the excitement of a hard fought, well-matched combat, one in which the primary weapons are the minds of the opponents.

The conflict begins before Seaton knows he has an enemy, when DuQuesne inspires World Steel to hire agents to steal a sample of the X solution from Crane's safe. Despite DuQuesne's advice, a careless Steel experimenter releases atomic energy in a burst, blasting a hole in the landscape. Seaton recognizes the source of the explosion, figures out that DuQuesne has, in Crane's words, "the brains, the ability, and the inclination" to have engineered the scheme (p. 84; not in revision), and, in a countermove, takes steps to have DuQuesne watched. For his part, DuQuesne leaves his dwelling by a secret passage. Seaton, however, has set a tracing device, an "object-compass," on DuQuesne and can monitor his movements (p. 100; p. 42). The game goes on. One has the advantage, then the other. DuQuesne arranges to have the construction of the Skylark sabotaged, while his own spaceship is being built, also dictating "that the craft should mount a couple of heavy guns, to destroy [the Skylark] if the faulty members should happen to hold together long enough to carry it out into space" (p. 111; not in revision); a few pages later, Seaton tells Crane, "'We might mount a machine-gun in every quadrant, shooting X-plosive bullets . . . . We should have something for defense--I don't like the possibility of having a gang of pirates after us, and nothing to fight back with'" (p. 113; p. 47, considerably revised). Later, the interaction becomes looser and more complicated, but this kind of brain-stretching matching of wits continues throughout the Skylark series.(6) When direct conflict between Seaton and DuQuesne is adjourned, it is replaced largely by similar conflict between Seaton and beings of races who think like DuQuesne. In the first novel, for example, the disembodied intelligence has clear affinities to DuQuesne in its contempt for human emotion and its stated pursuit of pure knowledge; that, after all, is why Seaton imagines DuQuesne can fit into the company of the intelligences at the end of Skylark DuQuesne, Smith even says that DuQuesne "had admired certain traits of Fenachrone character so much that he had gone en rapport with that engineer's mind practically cell to cell, with the result that he had emerged from that mental union as nearly a Fenachrone himself as a human could very well became" (p. 188).

If the Skylark novels are based on a constant process of dialectic rethinking, best seen in the conflict between Seaton and DuQuesne or one of his analogs, the effectiveness of some aspects of Smith's work can be appreciated more clearly.

One aspect was mentioned very vaguely a few pages ago as "the use of imagination." Others would call it "the sense of wonder." In any event, readers over the decades have spoken of the way Smith's writing communicates a sense of freshness, an anticipation of new things happening. As I have suggested, it is not simply the presence of unusual ideas that creates a sense of originality. The two samples of early science fiction noted earlier contain ideas that rival Smith's in wildness; yet they create less feeling of the imagination at work, and they involve the reader's imagination less. "The Planet Juggler" is full of events--so full that it reads like the condensed version of a full-length novel--but by and large the threats and discoveries are sprung on the reader so rapidly that they have little impact. And, as noted earlier, they all originate offstage. In "Crashing Suns," Hamilton hypes the action emotionally--the world of the monstrous globe-men is described as "a lurid world whose mountains, plains, and valleys were all of the same bloodlike hue as the light that fell upon them, whose very lakes and rivers gave back to the sky the scarlet tinge that pervaded all things here" (p. 22), and the globe-men unpleasantly suggest a race of blood-swollen ticks--but again there is little excitement. The objects described exist merely because they must fill out a pre-set plot; the enemies of Earth must be loathsome creatures living in a dreadful place.

In the Skylark novels, on the other hand, Smith manages to create convincing marvels because they appear unexpectedly, in plots that have the improvised feel of real experience, and because the characters must themselves really think about what happens. It is not the raw magnitude of the wonders, nor is it their natural verisimilitude that matters. Actually, Smith's public attitude toward scientific accuracy was surprisingly cavalier for someone appearing in the pages of an early science-fiction magazine. Replying to one query about the science in his work, Smith commented that he viewed the notion of curved space-time "as a theory . . . I declare it to be my privilege to violate it in any way I please in my fiction, even though I may believe in it as firmly as does my opponent."(7) He got away with it. Of all the people who wrote in to question some aspect of the science in the

25

Skylark novels, very few failed to couple their criticism with praise of the stories. For example, after calling attention to a number of dubious scientific statements in The Skylark of Space, John W. Campbell, Jr., concluded that "however, my personal opinion has always been that 'Skylark of Space' was the best story of scientifiction ever published, without exception. I have recently changed my opinion, however, since 'Skylark Three' has come out."(8) Actually, the sense of wonder is created by a writer's interest in what he is writing about. If he is interested in thinking about his subject, he stands at least a fair chance of involving a reader in it also. In Smith's case, the process of thinking, turning an idea over and over, building, extrapolating, is so basic in his fiction that it actively involves readers in the creation of wonders. It persuades even people who question the scientific bases of the events to enjoy the stories, since their becoming involved in the process of thinking makes the concepts impressive.

If the effect of Smith's depiction of dialectic extrapolation justifies the Skylark novels' apparently loose plotting, it also helps justify their prose style. In such an atmosphere, eloquent style is less than important; in fact, a flat statement of fact does not diminish involvement when it delivers its message and serves to provoke more thinking. The accelerating rush of ideas, not the style, is vital. As a result, levels of wonder are constantly growing stale--but Smith works this into his story also. One of the things much on Smith's mind, obviously, was the exciting prospect of freely exploring the universe. Smith states this several times, as Seaton stays awake early in The Skylark of Space, thinking about the prospect of spaceflight (p. 28; not in revision). However, in Skylark Three, Seaton comments, "'Well, we're here, folks, on another new world. Not quite as thrilling as the first one was, is it?'" (p. 143; p. 124). Nevertheless, Seaton and his party are welcomed to Norlamin with an enthusiastic declaration of how much is left to experience, even for the Norlaminians: "'The more we know, the vaster the virgin fields of investigation opened to us'" (p. 135; p. 117). Smith generally stresses how small humanity is in the scheme of the universe, yet pulls his characters to a stop before they can much lament human weakness; he believes, as Margaret says in The Skylark of Space, that "'there is something in man as great as all this'" (p. 181; p. 84). And so the characters continue onward, eager for the next surprise, the next challenge.

It follows naturally that Smith stresses openness to new experiences and ideas. Seaton approaches each new race

willing to be friends and to learn. He is especially recep-
tive to the idea of nudity, which appears on Osnome in the
first book and recurs through most of the human culture the
Tellurians encounter. He also listens receptively to the
different moral codes offered by each alien culture. Though
he does not put them into practice as fast as he adapts to
nudity--and though some of the comments on religion,
marriage, and politics may simply show Smith poking fun at
contemporary targets--Seaton does not reject out of hand the
idea of racial development by mental tests to regulate
selective breeding. At the same time, a closer study of
Smith's work shows that he is not advocating the human-
chauvinist lunacy that some critics charge. Brian
Stableford's essay-review of the Skylark series in Survey of
Science Fiction Literature, for example, attacks Smith for
thoughtlessly wiping out alien races with the cry '"Humanity
uber alles."(9) But the working definition of "humanity" in
the series is actually broad enough to include any being who
will admit that other beings have a right to exist freely.
The physically humanoid Fenachrones are less sympathetic
than the Llurdi; the latter can use their minds so effi-
ciently that they can make peace with the Jelmi as soon as
the humanoids demonstrate that they are more than
inherently-inferior slaves. In fact, the two races can
think so much alike that one of the Jelmi remarks to her
mate that "'you know I almost like--I actually admire that
horrible monster in some ways!'" (SDQ, p. 173). The key,
not surprisingly, is the type of intelligence an alien race
shows: "humans" must be able to think in an incremental,
problem-solving fashion rather than rigidly applying a set
formula (such as absolute racial superiority); they also
must be able to recognize when another being of whatever
shape shares that kind of intelligence. That is humanity.
That is the ideal Smith maintains to the death against all
beings who must enslave others because they have enslaved
and perverted their own intelligences.

If this helps explain the basis of Smith's ideas and
the way he gave them believability and excitement, it also
helps explain what he did by way of creating characters.

Essentially, Smith spends little time building complex
characters who can show a full range of doubts, weaknesses,
struggles against temptation, etc. Such things may be part
of the richest human triumphs, but they can lead to human
failures, too. Smith evidently does not consider them
necessary to his purpose. Most of the characters have no
chance to show much complexity, since they just say their
lines, contribute their bits of information, and leave the
stage. Continuing characters have some chance to do more.

27

Initially, Dorothy and Margaret look like conventional female stereotypes from the popular magazines. Essentially, they give decorative touches and patient understanding to the lives of their husbands. When, infrequently, they contribute something directly to the action, it is a bit of practical, down-to-earth thinking that untangles the complexities that beset the men (for example, see SV, pp. 95-96; pp. 81-82). In the last book of the series, this changes a bit, and the women insist on standing beside their men in the struggle. Still, though this adds another dimension to the women it does not add much complexity. Rather than the full range of human nature, the finished characters show two extremes, nothing between.

The same could be said of the male characters. Richard Seaton, in particular, shows two extremes: heartily good-natured extrovert and brilliant thinker. Between those extremes, there is very little sense of personality. Fortunately, the two extremes are striking enough to be interesting. Seaton's analytic turn of mind, coupled with Smith's primary concern for the process of thinking, hits the reader vividly. The other side, the ring-tailed roarer from the West, is a bit startling when it burst out, but it is strikingly done, too; here is Seaton, sounding for all the world like Davy Crockett or Mike Fink, as he bids DuQuesne goodbye at the end of The Skylark of Space:

> "Go as far as you like," Seaton answered cheerfully. "If we're not a match for you and your gang, on foot or in the air, in body or in mind, we'll deserve whatever we get. We can outrun you, outjump you, throw you down, or lick you; we can run faster, hit harder, dive deeper, and come up dryer, than you can. We'll play any game you want to deal; for fun, money, chalk, or marbles. Hop to it!" (p. 301; p. 157, somewhat abridged)

The male characters in the Skylark novels also have some sense of complexity otherwise lacking in Smith's work because he sets them up to complement each other, so that one displays traits that another lacks. To understand the full range of characterization, one thus needs to observe how various characters illustrate different sides of human nature. Smith states this most directly in the case of Seaton and Crane, the former supplying energy and inspiration while the latter contributes steadiness and practical suggestions. But the most striking example of paired characterization is that of Seaton and DuQuesne. The two are almost perfect mirror images of each other. In physique, they are so similar that DuQuesne can pose as Seaton in a raid on Crane's home (SS, p. 93; p. 39). Seaton is slightly superior in their one direct competition in The Skylark of Space. Mentally, they are approximately equal. DuQuesne himself comments, while waiting for his spaceship to fall into the dark sun, that he hopes Seaton survives because the release of atomic energy "'is the greatest discovery the world has ever seen; and if Seaton and I, the only two men in the world who know how to handle it, drop out, it will be lost, perhaps for hundreds of years'" (SS, p. 154; p. 69). Again, in their frequent mental duels, Seaton has a slight edge.

More important, though, are the differences between the two. Seaton is light in coloring, DuQuesne dark. Seaton uses slang frequently, while DuQuesne speaks more formal, correct English (at least in the opening books of the series). Seaton enjoys the company of others and relies on trust and friendship in dealing with co-workers. DuQuesne is quite comfortable alone, though he will take along assistants whenever he needs them as long as he can control them completely by power or greed. In fact, looking back at DuQuesne's attitude toward the development of X and his excitement at working out a scientific problem, it appears that the major difference between the two is their attitudes toward others. Seaton is good and DuQuesne is evil because the latter works in isolation. They share the same zeal to explore and master; DuQuesne simply pursues his goals with selfish excess. He is an alternative version of Seaton, the reverse of the scientist as an open, uninhibited human being.

Still, for a reader, DuQuesne is not utterly unsympathetic. Like Milton's Satan or Stevenson's Long John Silver, he is admirable in the singleminded purity of his selfishness. Moreover, DuQuesne can be counted on to cut through pretense of romance. He knows exactly what he wants, and he is impatient with pretense by people he thinks are pursuing similar ends. He is a refreshingly cold-hearted villain.

In each of the first three Skylark novels, Smith tries to dispose of DuQuesne--by sending him off with a fortune and a vague hint of reformation in the first novel, incinerating him in the second, and kicking his soul out of the universe in the third. It never works. At the end of The Skylark of Space, like the end of Treasure Island, the fascinating but utterly untrustworthy rogue must be allowed to escape. In each succeeding book, however, Smith cannot do without DuQuesne as a complement of Seaton. His kinship

to Seaton can never be acknowledged, but his presence can
never be obliterated either.

The fact that Smith keeps trying to obliterate DuQuesne
shows that he wanted to end the conflict between the sides
of human nature in simple triumph of the Good. It also
shows that he wanted to finish the story of the Skylarks, to
tie up everything in a knot. The magazine version of
Skylark Three shows how determined he was, ending with an
epilogue that (as far as I know) has never been reprinted:

> The three-dimensional, moving talking, al-
> most living picture, being shown simultaneously
> in all the viewing areas throughout the in-
> numerable planets of the galaxy, faded out and
> the image of an aged, white-bearded Norlaminian
> appeared and spoke in the Galactic language.
> "As is customary, the showing of this picture
> has opened the celebration of our great Galactic
> holiday, Civilization Day. As you all know, it
> portrays the events leading up to and making
> possible the formation of the League of Planets
> by a mere handful of planets. The League now
> embraces all of this, the First Galaxy, and is
> spreading rapidly throughout the Universe.
> Varied are the physical forms and varied are the
> mentalities of our almost innumerable races of
> beings, but in Civilization we are becoming one,
> since those backward people who will not
> cooperate with us are rendered impotent to im-
> pede our progress among the more enlightened."
> "It is peculiarly fitting that the one who
> has just been chosen to head the Galactic
> Council--the first person of a race other than
> one of those of the Central System to prove him-
> self able to wield justly the vast powers of
> office--should be a direct descendant of two of
> the revered persons whose deeds of olden times
> we have just witnessed."
> "I present to you my successor as Chief of
> the Galactic Council, Richard Ballinger Seaton,
> the fourteenth hundred sixty-nine, of
> Earth."(10)

That certainly finishes off the series. Or so it must
have seemed. Soon, however, readers were calling for
sequels, perhaps featuring descendants of Richard and
Dorothy. Smith replied:

> I did end the "Skylark" stories, definitely,
> purposefully; so that you would all know that
> they were done. In fact, I did not expect to
> hear a single request for more. However, there
> have been some such request, and if there are
> enough more, I will try again. There are
> several ways of getting away from that
> epilogue.(11)

What made it possible for Smith to ignore the epilogue and
untie the knot that ended the characters' adventures was not
simply the readers' demands for more. Rather, as suggested
throughout this chapter, the heart of the Skylark series in
particular and Smith's work in general is the human mind's
attempt to extend itself, to think through ideas and overcome problems. As Smith consciously concluded each Skylark
novel, wrapping up the plot for once and for all, what could
be more natural than that he also should be trying to think
his way past the conclusion, imaging how that set of difficulties could be overcome?

As a series, the Skylark novels grew by accretion
rather than conscious design. Smith himself was so unsure
that he had finished everything in Skylark of Valeron that
he simply sent off the rough manuscript to F. Orlin
Tremaine, editor of Astounding, with a request for
suggestions. Tremaine published the story as it stood, and
in fact it seems no looser in structure than the other
novels. Like them, it succeeds because of its driving
energy that is focused through Smith's abiding interest in
characters trying to solve problems, to make sense of a
potentially chaotic situation.

In Skylark DuQuesne, finally, Smith moved closer to ac-
cepting the open-ended form that the Skylark stories
naturally used. True, that novel is billed as the last of
the series. So was Skylark of Valeron. So was Skylark
Three, earlier still. In fact, the situation at the end of
Skylark DuQuesne is the least settled of any of the novels.
A crew of the Fenachrone is free, in possession of much
technological power. The Llurdi are convinced for the moment that they should not interfere with humans, but this
holds true as long as there is no logical advantage in their
tampering. Above all, DuQuesne is free, with a mighty
spaceship of his own and a plan to form an empire based on
his values. And those are merely the known potential
hazards.

At the end of Skylark DuQuesne, DuQuesne states his intention to leave the "soft" worlds that suit the likes of
Seaton and build his own regime. There should be no need

for him ever to seek contact with his former adversaries. But does there have to be a "need?" At the end of Skylark of Valeron, just before he imprisons DuQuesne's spirit with the disembodied intelligences, Seaton sums up his judgment of the man: "He'd never be satisfied unless he was all three rings of the circus. Being a big shot isn't enough-- he's got to be the Poo-Bah. He's naturally anti-social--he would always be making trouble and would never fit into a really civilized world'" (pp. 248-249; pp. 202-203). It might seem that DuQuesne's plans at the end of Skylark DuQuesne would give him a perfect chance to be the Poo-Bah; however, his earlier career, summed up by Seaton, does not suggest that he can ever be content to dominate any limited area. Unreformed, in full possession of his talents and of much power, DuQuesne certainly is set up for further con- flict in some future, unwritten Skylark novel.(12)

The only way to deny the existence of this threat is to accept something that opens up the conclusion of the series even more. Seaton's judgment may be wrong. It happens repeatedly in Skylark DuQuesne. In fact, one of the novel's points is that there are always wild, unpredictable factors that break certainties. Every time one of the characters in the novel settles back, content that he has figured out something he can rely on, Smith informs the reader that this is a mistake. As Smith comments near the middle of the novel,

> The events in this climactic struggle between
> arch-enemies, Seaton and DuQuesne, were at this
> point reaching an area of maximum tension. It
> is curious to reflect that the outer symptom of
> this internal disruptive stress was, in the case
> of nearly every major component of the events to
> come, a psychological state of either satisfied
> achievement, or contented decision, or calm
> resignation. It is as though each of the major
> operatives were suffering from a universe-wide
> sense of false tranquility (p. 165).

Certainly the climax of Skylark DuQuesne, in which psionics destroys the Chlorans, is the wildest, least intel- ligible card of all. But it still plays well. One mark of the scientist, remember, is that he can recognize when some- thing out of the ordinary is present--and usable. In the last book of the Skylark series, Smith again is opening up a new area for exploration. That should not be unexpected. From the first novel, one of DuQuesne's weaknesses has been his tendency to explain too much, to deny the possibility of accident, as when he supposed that X was an invention of Seaton's that the other had deliberately concealed (SS, p. 45; p. 22). It may be that, having once toyed with the idea of scientific dictatorship and controlled breeding, Smith is finally willing to let DuQuesne demonstrate what that kind of rigid control can and cannot accomplish. Such testing of the limits of human control at all levels is one of the possibilities left open in the Skylark series.

Skylark DuQuesne does show that opportunities for balance and unity are a great deal more complex than in the earlier novels. The psionic force at the end emerges from many, various individuals. Even DuQuesne contributes his part, pushing ruthlessly ahead when Seaton falters (pp. 230-232). The need to accept and respect the separateness of individuals is as pressing now as it ever has been, and its potentially galaxy-shaping power is waiting. The need to strain human ability to comprehend and control the things that one encounters on each level of growth remains. Humans are tiny things. Their knowledge is a minute, pathetic glimmer in the midst of infinite darkness. Yet they have the ability to extend themselves by thinking, coupled with intuition and energy.

Smith does not resolve these issues. Perhaps he could not have in an infinite number of Skylark novels. But he does raise them vividly, and he does involve readers in the process of reaching, imaging, straining ever outward into the unknown.

NOTES

(1) Amazing Stories, August 1928, p. 390.
(2) Discussed in Redd Boggs, "Flight of the Skylarks," Spaceship, No. 25 (June 1954).
(3) Beginning publication in 1923, Weird Tales actually published a mixture of fantasy and science-fiction, and it continued to do so for several years after the appearance of specialized science-fiction magazines. Hamilton's short novel eventually was published in book form in the collection Crashing Suns (New York: Ace, 1965).
(4) P. 524
(5) (New York: Ace, 1964).
(6) In Skylark Three, for example, Seaton corrects an earlier error with the comment--
          "Remember that planet we struck on the first trip, that had an atmosphere composed mostly of gaseous chlorine? In our ignorance we assumed that life there was

impossible, and didn't stop. Well, it may
be just as well that we didn't. If we go
back there, protected as we are with our
screens and stuff, it wouldn't surprise me
a bit to find life there, and lots of it—
and I've got a hunch that it'll be a form
of life that'd make your grandfather's
whiskers curl right up into a ball!" (pp.
130-131; p. 111).
—picking up an idea from The Skylark of Space and
preparing for Skylark of Valeron.

(7) "Discussions [letter column], Amazing Stories. April
     1931, p. 96.
(8) "Discussions," Amazing Stories, September 1930, p.
     568.
(9) Volume Five (Englewood Cliffs, NJ: Salem, 1979), 2093.
(10) Amazing Stories, October 1930, p. 658.
(11) "Discussions," Amazing Stories, April 1931, p. 96.
(12) In his discussion of his years as a science-fiction
     editor, Frederik Pohl clearly implies that he expected
     Smith to write more Skylark adventures (Yesterday's
     Tomorrows [New York: Berkley, 1982], p. 407).

V

THE LENSMEN SERIES: SMITH'S "EPIC OF SPACE"

After completing, as he then supposed, the Skylark series with "Skylark of Valeron" in 1934, Smith began a quite different type of work. From the evolving, piecemeal Skylark novels, Smith turned to a project that he had been developing for close to a decade: the Lensmen saga. As he explains in his essay "The Epic of Space," he began thinking of doing a "space-police novel" shortly after Amazing Stories accepted the manuscript of "Skylark of Space."(1) For a time he grappled with the technical extrapolation that he needed to permit action to take place on an inter-galactic scale. This seemed altogether unworkable until Smith came upon the idea of doing away with spaceships' inertia so that they could achieve faster-than-light speeds, a notion he admits is just this side of absolute mathematical impossibility. He then tackled the problem of intergalactic communication, at the same time pondering "the apparent impossibility of having my policemen invent or develop an identifying symbol which all good citizens would recognize but which malefactors could not counterfeit" (p. 84). Solving both problems with the concept of the Lens, Smith finished laying out the Lensmen universe. Only then did he turn to possible literary models, reading as much police science fiction as he could to see what other writers had done with the theme. He wrote to F. Orlin Tremaine, editor of Astounding Stories, at this point, asking whether it would be advisable to go ahead with his own cops-and-robbers story. With Tremaine's enthusiastic encouragement, Smith proceeded to draw up a detailed outline, working from the natural laws of his universe through the eons-long struggle between the Arisians and the Eddorians to the centerstage characters who perform the action.

One thing Smith discovered very early in his outlining was that it would take more than one book to tell the story. Much more. He planned four long stories ("Galactic Patrol," "Gray Lensman," "Second Stage Lensmen," and "Children of the Lens"). Eventually, he would work "Triplanetary," an Amazing serial of early 1934, into the beginning of the Lensmen fabric, and he would add First Lensmen to bridge the gap between that new opening book and the originally-conceived four books that deal with the exploits of Kim Kinnison. He also would write the "Vortex Blaster" stories (set in the Lensmen universe but having no relation to the main plot) as a sidebar series. Still, it is important to note that the books Smith added later to the body of the series are prequels, giving preliminary information, not sequels adding to what he already had planned. The original conception held firm.(2) Though it is called a series, the Lensmen saga is one, unified, coherent work; as Smith says, "it is in reality one story."

It is difficult to appreciate the imaginative courage of Smith's effort from our perspective of half a century later. We have seen many endless science-fiction series, racing nowhere at great speed and designed never to conclude as long as readers don't get bored. We also have become used to seeing limited series or multi-volume novels—such as Asimov's Foundation series or Farmer's Riverworld—whose writers have a stopping place in mind but allow themselves several hundred thousand words to develop their story. Smith did not have our advantages. He could observe how a template series was put together, but he had no models of the latter type of work on which to base his project. He was forced to proceed on his own. He was certain that he did not want to do the kind of glamorous, picturesque adventures in which Edgar Rice Burroughs specialized. Whether in deliberate revolt against that kind of haphazard structuring or not, but certainly using his experience in writing the Skylark novels, Smith planned his four-volume Lensmen novel in detail. He made sure he had his basic purpose clear, and then he let the story develop in detail it needed. This was a unique, breathtaking accomplishment inside the science-fiction field; as far as I know, the Lensmen saga is the very first multivolume science-fiction novel. Long before the days of paperback promotions—before a science-fiction writer could even count on his novel being reprinted after it had been serialized in a magazine—Smith had the nerve to plan a story as large as his imagination could stretch and then to settle down to write it as fully as he felt it deserved.

With his overall framework, Smith still left room for a great deal of spontaneity in the actual writing. He prepared some six-hundred pages of background information, including calculations of the math and physics involved. He also prepared detailed dramatic outlines of the novels. The one for "Galactic Patrol," for example, showed not only the events but the growing emotional intensity, the careful introduction of background and characterization during relatively slack times in the action, etc.: "each [emotional] peak was a bit higher than the one before, as was each valley floor, until the climax was reached; after which the graph descended abruptly" (p. 86). However, after wryly

noting how beautiful his charts are before he begins
writing, Smith adds, "Unfortunately, . . . while I can't
seem to work without something of the kind, I have never yet
been able to follow one at all closely. My characters get
away from me and do exactly as they damn please" (p.86).

Smith's writing is, in fact, a mixture of careful
preparation and often-fortuitous improvisation. But the two
support each other beautifully in the Lensmen novels. We
already have seen how Smith's grappling with the problem of
intergalactic communication led him to imagine the Lens, an
augmenter of telephathic talents. I suspect that the feed-
back between grasping a concept and leaping past it was more
complex and continuous than that. To produce the Lens,
Smith had to imagine the Arisians; to imagine why a race
capable of producing the Lens would produce it and give it
to necessarily inferior creatures. he had to imagine the
Arisians as important elements on the side of Good in its
struggle against Evil and had to fit that struggle into his
story. To make the novels, in the long run, more than the
simple cops-and-robbers stories that he already knew and
would have been bored trying to recreate, he had to involve
his characters in the attack on the true source of Evil.
And he had to imagine how possession of the Lens would af-
fect his characters. It would be wrong to imagine that
Smith was merely a meticulous organizer, too set in his
preparations to allow any free growth in the actual heat of
writing. It also would be wrong to imagine that Smith was
merely a spontaneous story teller, who rambled through tale
after tale because he lacked skill to do anything better.
He was both a planner and an improviser, and the two aspects
of his talent worked together very productively in the
Lensmen series.

Before we see how Smith skillfully structured the whole
Lensmen series for maximum effect and then examine some sections in detail, let us review the work's sweeping plot.

The basis of the entire story is the intersection, approximately two billion years ago, of two galaxies, producing stresses that created many planetary systems where
before there had been only a few in each galaxy. Thus, the
intelligent race already existing in each galaxy found itself with a myriad of potentially habitable solar systems
waiting for development. As it happened, one race was the
Arisians and the other the Eddorians; for reasons I will explain later, they represent, respectively, Good and Evil.
The Arisians became aware of the Eddorians first. They
realized that, although they could block awareness of their
presence from the Eddorians, they could not totally defeat
their nemesis. They thus began a long-term campaign of en-

couraging the evolution of life to their ends, while the Eddorians began their attempts to corrupt and destroy any positive developments they were aware of.

At the beginning of Triplanetary, six chapters added to the book version explain this conflict and show it being waged throughout human history. Each time they intervene, the Eddorians succeed. Atlantis sinks, Rome is debased, corruption seethes in America during World War II, etc. Moreover, Smith shows how limited human beings are by their preconceptions. In the section showing Nero's Rome, one positive character reacts to the news that hundreds of Christians are about to be crucified with the comment "'Why not? Everyone knows that they are poisoners of wells and murderers of children and practitioners of magic . . .'" and the hero replies, "'True enough'" and shrugs (p. 38; p. 41). Still, Gharlane, the Eddorian who monitors Tellus--and sometimes acts directly in human form--is puzzled at how fast the humans recover from their setbacks and learn to do better. Unknown to him, a certain type of intelligent heroism, associated in modern times with the name Kinnison, is surviving and developing; it must work within human limitations, but it is stretching those limitations. After inducing World War III, Gharlane turns his attention away from the solar system for a time--and Arisia-influenced humanity pulls itself together, begins exploring space, and forms a league of Venus, Mars, and Tellus after a war with Jupiter.

The main plot of Triplanetary--the novel itself as first serialized in Amazing in 1934--begins with space pirates seizing a passenger liner and delivering the three survivors--Captain Bradley, secret agent Conway Costigan, and lovely Clio Marsden--to the pirate chief, Gray Roger (actually, Smith explained in the revision, Gharlane of Eddore). With Costigan's spy devices (and an assist from the Arisians, who block Gharlane at a crucial moment), the three escape from the pirate base, only to be snared by an exploring warship from the solar system of Nevia. Nerado of Nevia, commander of the expedition, has come searching for supplies of iron, a rare metal on his water-covered world, and he destroys Roger's planetoid (along with the fleet from the Triplanetary League attacking it) and returns home with Costigan, Bradley, and Clio Marsden as biological specimens. During an attack on the amphibious Nevians by fish-creatures from deeper in the ocean, the humans escape in a small spaceship but are soon recaptured and brought back to Nevia. In the meantime, the Triplanetary Service, aided by information Costigan broadcast earlier, has developed counters to the Nevians weapons and installed them in an experimental, inertialess-drive super spaceship, the <u>Boise</u>. When it is damaged after driving a Nevian ship away from an iron-gathering attack on Philadelphia, the <u>Boise</u> settles down on a nearby planet for repairs—and stumbles on Gray Roger rebuilding his planetoid, wiping out the pirates once and for all. (Actually, Gharlane simply returns home, to scheme with the Innermost Council of Eddore.) Meanwhile, Costigan has managed to manufacture a supply of the same gas the pirates used on the spaceliner at the story's beginning. He releases it, killing a city full of the amphibians, and races away toward Tellus again. This time, the humans are picked up by the <u>Boise,</u> which destroys one Nevian warship and a huge Nevian city. Finally, the two races negotiate a peace treaty, recognizing that their previous antagonism was due to hasty misunderstanding.

The next novel, <u>First Lensman,</u> connects <u>Triplanetary</u> with the Lensmen books by showing how characters from the first novel form the Galactic Patrol and begin learning what it means to be a Lensman. <u>First Lensman</u> was first published as a hardcover book in 1950. In this novel, Arisia overtly enters the struggle against the enemies of Civilization for the first time. The novel begins with Gharlane attempting to assassinate Dr. Nels Bergenholm, actually the manifestation of an Arisian, who twits the Eddorian about Arisia's well-laid plans. When Virgil Samms, chief of the Triplanetarian Secret Service, is puzzled how to find an un-forgeable identity badge for his agents, "Bergenholm" advises him to go to Arisia. The Arisians give Samms the first Lens. Physically, the Lens is a shimmering disk, worn on the wrist of its one, unique, superior male owner.(3) In addition to identifying its wearer as a superior warrior for Civilization, the Lens gives him telepathic powers (and hints of other abilities), though actually "a Lens has no power of its own; it merely concentrates, intensifies, and renders available whatever powers are already possessed by its wearer" (<u>FL</u>, p. 36; pp. 32-33). In the rest of the novel, Samms must work on two fronts to achieve his goal of turning the Triplanetarian Service into an agency capable of policing the reaches of space now open to humans—a Galactic Patrol. He must find individuals capable of wearing the Lens, and he takes the first steps in recognizing that alien races may possess qualities that qualify them to be Lensmen. He also must stabilize a degenerating society on Tellus. Under Samms' direction, the new Lensmen begin separate, secret investigations of political corruption (Operation Mateese), drugs and vice (Operation Zwilnik), and space piracy (Operation Boskone). Actually, the three turn out to come from the same roots (and the latter two turn out to

require such long struggle that their names enter the
language, meaning "drug dealer or criminal" and "the enemy
organization," respectively). Following an attempt on his
life and an attack by the pirate fleet on his headquarters,
Samms becomes an underground agent and burrows his way
toward the top of the drug smuggling organization. His
friend and assistant, Rod Kinnison, is elected President,
and the government is falling safely into the hands of the
Lensmen so they can continue their efforts to build a
genuinely free Civilization throughout the universe.

The next four novels were the ones planned by Smith as
a unit. They were the ones printed by Astounding as the
Lensmen series, and until the publication of the revised
form of Triplanetary and first publication of First Lensman,
they were the Lensmen series. Keep in mind that the first
readers of these novels had none of the background explained
in the first two novels. They did not know, for example,
the true nature of Arisia, let alone the mere existence of
Eddore. Like the Lensmen themselves, readers were forced to
figure out things as the action developed.

Galactic Patrol (serialized in Astounding, September
1937-February 1938) begins with the graduation of Kimball
Kinnison at the head of his class of candidates for the Lens
of the Galactic Patrol. Almost immediately, Kim is sent on
a mission to snare one of the new spaceships of the pirates
of Boskone, so that he can bring back information about
their new power system. He is successful in capturing the
pirate ship, but he decides to split up his crew and scatter
in his ship's lifeboats to increase the chances of getting
the information back to Tellus. Kim and Peter Van Buskirk,
a massive warrior from the heavy-gravity planet Valeria,
hijack a disabled Boskonian ship, then try to elude pursuit
by dropping off in an unknown solar system. There, on the
planet Delgon, they are rescued from attacking animals by
the reptilian Worsel of Valentia III, whom they aid in
destroying a nest of Overlords, telepathic superhypnotists
who have been summoning Valentians so they can torture them
to death and feed on their agonized life forces. With the
Valentians' aid, Kim summons the surviving members of his
crew and traps several Boskonian warships, again escaping in
several directions on his mission toward home. He barely
beats the enemy back to Tellus. His experience has given
him some new ideas for space-battle tactics, the realization
that Boskone is a whole culture of its own rather than a
rabble of disaffected Tellurians as had previously been
believed--and one line tracking the source of a message from
what appears to be the enemy's high command, "'Helmuth,
speaking for Boskone.'" Using Kim's suggestions, the Patrol

seizes an advantage over Boskone; then the enemy makes
adjustments, and a stalemate develops. Meanwhile, however,
Kim has developed a shield to hide his small space ship from
detection, and he trails a pirate ship to its base.
Unfortunately, he is detected at the base and is severely
wounded; fortunately, he is nursed back to health by
Clarissa MacDougall, a descendant of Virgil Samms, who is as
splendid a specimen of humanity as Kim is. Realizing that
he is less able than he should be, Kim makes an unprece-
dented second trip to Arisia, where he goes through mind-
stretching training that gives him the power to control
other minds, perceive without using his eyes, etc. So
prepared, he invades a pirate base and saves Clarissa and a
group of other captured nurses from rape, drawing a second
tracer line on Helmuth in the process. Having now located
the enemy's major base, he acquires a massive supply of the
euphoric drug thionite and approaches Helmuth's
headquarters, where he takes control of the unshielded mind
of a dog and manipulates the animal to disconnect the
thought shield of one defender, spreads his control through
several humans, circulates thionite through the air supply,
and calls down an attack by the Patrol's fleet in the midst
of the confusion. Kim and Helmuth grapple during the
battle, and the latter is killed.

Supposedly, thus, Boskone is finished; Kim commented,
just before the final battle, that "'I'm just as sure that
Helmuth is Boskone as I can be of anything that can't be
proved'" (GP, p. 254; p. 219). As often happens in the
Lensmen novels, however, this certainty is false. The story
continues in Gray Lensman (serialized in Astounding, October
1939-January 1940), beginning with the revelation that
during their hand-to-hand combat Kim got some jumbled
glimpses of Helmuth's thoughts suggesting that the latter
reported to someone else higher inside Boskone. When he
traces the new line of communication outside the galaxy, Kim
realizes the Boskone's real base must be more powerful than
he had imagined. Before he can pursue that lead, he is
honored for the work already done and finds himself
naturally falling into mental unity with Clarissa
MacDougall; the two part, each feeling unworthy of the
other's love. On a preliminary mission to the nearby galaxy
where Boskone seems to be based, Kim and his crew encounter
the space-driven planet Medon, fleeing from the Boskonian
forces that dominate the entire galaxy. This inspires Kim
with the notion of using whole, powered planets as weapons.
He also comes to realize that although Boskone's military
arm (piracy) has been disrupted in the Patrol's home galaxy,
the subversion and domination arm (drugs) is still

operative. Accordingly, he devotes most of his time to tracing the drug supply to its source, confident that it will get him to the new headquarters of Boskone. He goes underground, posing first as a gentleman of leisure, then as a dock-walloper, to trace the zwilnik operation on the planet Bronsica. While this is going on, the cold-blooded Eich, a council of whom replaced Helmuth as spokesman for Boskone, debate the nature of the force opposing them; they attempt to spy out Arisia but are thwarted and taunted. At a temporary standstill in his investigation, Kim supervises the creation of the negasphere, a ball of negative matter intended to be used as a weapon, then takes the role of asteroid miner to pick up another line on the drug traffic. This imposture is interrupted when Patrol ships are attacked by invisible, mind-controlling foes; Kim, Worsel, and Van Buskirk figure out that the attackers must be surviving Overlords of Delgon, but they are almost overcome when the Overlords attack by surprise through a hyper-spatial tube. After disposing of the obscene monsters, Kim leads an attack through the tube that cripples a Boskonian base. Back at work as a spy, Kim finally discovers the location of the zwilnik home base in the Second Galaxy. He and Worsel travel there, and Kim explores the base; however, he is caught and hideously tortured before the Eich turn their attention away from him and Worsel is able to get him back to Tellus. There, Clarissa MacDougall declares her love, Kim protests that he will not have her tied to a maimed monstrosity--but a new technique of regeneration restores him to normal. To wipe out Boskone once and for all, though, Kim supervises the destruction of the main zwilnik outpost in the First Galaxy (devoured by negaspheres) and directs the later attack on the home world of the Eich (crushed and burst between two powered planets). His task accomplished, he returns to Clarissa, and they walk toward a justly-deserved, long-anticipated life together.

. . . . until the mood is shattered a split second later, at the beginning of Second Stage Lensmen (Astounding, November 1941-February 1942): "'Stop, Youth!' The voice of Mentor the Arisian thundered silently, deep within the Lensman's brain. . . . 'At times, Kinnison of Tellus, we almost despair of you. Think, Youth, think!'" (p. 17; p. 21). After a brief explosion of frustration, Kim does think, whereupon he realizes that Boskone may not have been completely wiped out--and that the Boskonians are capable of duplicating the Galactic Patrol's weapons. Accordingly, he plans a hurried defense that thwarts a Boskonian attack that launches planets at Tellus through a hyper-spatial tube. Then, reshouldering his burden of responsibility, Kim again traces zwilnik operations. This time he pursues a young female zwilnik Illona to the previously uncharted First Galaxy planet Lyrane, whose thinking race is entirely female. Capturing Illona, Kim converts her to the side of Civilization and probes her mind for information about the Boskone-ruled world Lonabar. Disguised as a master criminal, he travels to Lonabar and baits the planet's ruler into trying to kill him in person, whereupon Kim probes that worthy's mind and kills him. In the meantime, with Arisia's approval, he has found time to train Clarissa (Chris) as a Lensman and has sent her to Lyrane. He and the other Second Stage Lensmen (those who have made a second trip to Arisia and been pushed into the next stage of mental mastery) confer with Chris and determine that a nest of Overlords must have been established on Lyrane, and they gleefully massacre the Overlords just in time to save the planet's ruler. With the information they are accumulating, the Lensmen begin to draw near the Boskonian headquarters in the Second Galaxy. While Nadreck of Palain VII, a poison-breathing Second State Lensman who resembles the Eich physically but whose heart (figuratively speaking) is with Civilization, begins a psychological attack that eventually will wipe out the planet-sized base Onlo, Kim takes the place of a low-level military officer on the central Boskonian planet Thrale. By superior intelligence, skill, and arrogance, he maneuvers his way to the top of the government, where he discovers that the prime minister Fossten is actually the all-controlling, thoroughly mind-shielded commander of the Boskonian forces. After a brief leave to try to explore a Boskonian hyperspace tube—during which Kim and his crew are dumped into another dimension and rescued only by mental advice from the Arisians—Kim replaces the current Tyrant of Thrale and builds an immense war fleet to attack Civilization. As the Boskonian fleet goes into battle, burdened by a fatal lack of coordination and the fact that Kim has been relaying all its plans to the Patrol, Kim becomes certain that Fossten actually is Boskone and engages in a desperate mental struggle with him. Finally convinced that he sees the other's true form—a giant Arisian brain—Kim strikes it, and the other loses consciousness. Mentor explains that Boskone was a renegade, insane Arisian, and the creature is destroyed. (Actually, it is explained in Children of the Lens, it is Gharlane of Eddore whom Kim defeats, with a boost of mental power from Arisia.) Following the destruction of the Boskonian fleet, Kim supervises the beginning of the pacification of the Second Galaxy, in particular the conversion of Thrale to a guided democracy. Then he returns to Earth and marries Chris, in a glow of well-deserved satisfaction.

At the beginning of Children of the Lens (Astounding, November 1947-February 1948), some twenty years have passed. Kim and Chris have had five children: a son, Christopher, and two sets of twins, Kathryn and Karen, Camilia and Constance. Kim, now Galactic Coordinator, is troubled by spreading outbreaks of crime and anti-social madness; there seems no pattern to this, but Kim suspects the power of Boskone is recovering. His children are certain of it. As the beginning of Triplanetary showed, the Arisians have been supervising two human bloodlines, culminating in Kim Kinnison and Clarissa MacDougall. Their children are Lensmen from birth, Second Stage Lensmen by the time the story opens, Third Stage Lensmen from fairly early in the action—and that is only the beginning. At the same time, just as the Arisians have stayed in the background as much as possible to avoid giving the younger races of Civilization an inferiority complex, the Kinnison children keep the full extent of their powers hidden. This means that the plot of Children of Lens is virtually impossible to summarize simply, for everything must be seen on at least two levels. First of all, on the level with which readers are familiar, Kim Kinnison, Chris (now raised to Second Stage Lensman), and the alien Second Stage Lensmen work their way through various traps laid for them by a Boskonian command structure that existed parallel to the system obliterated earlier. On this level, the action climaxes with the destruction of Boskone's new ultimate headquarters on the planet Ploor, followed by Kim's rescue from the Hell Hole of Space, an enemy trap prepared especially for him.

On the second level of reading, the reader watches as the Kinnison children attach themselves as protectors to the adults and nudge them through the dangers they must face. In the process, the children make enough mistakes to remind them that they need more training; the Arisians give them enough mind stretching to make them aware of their abilities but leave them with the realization that they are responsible for their own further development since their powers are beyond even Arisian comprehension. The effect of this multi-leveled storytelling is seldom merely ironic. The heroism of Kim, Chris, Worsel, Nadreck, and Tergonsee is not diminished by the help they unknowingly receive; their courage remains, complemented by the tactful affection of their cohorts. By the same token, the Children's errors do not diminish their ability; they learn from them and grow past them. On the second level, then, the story moves through various preliminary adventures, through the destruction of Ploor, on to the attack on Eddore (its existence never suspected by the others) that combines the powers of the Children and a burst of power borrowed from all Lensmen's minds, and to the recovery of Kim from the distant continuum where the Hell Hole transported him, which is followed by the departure of the Arisians from this plane of existence after they have appointed the Children their replacements as Guardians of Civilization.

It is the third-level effect of Children of the Lens and of the Lensmen novels as a whole--the way Smith involves the reader in the action and his purpose in doing so--that will be discussed in the remainder of this chapter. It is worth discussing. Despite its immense bulk and the frantic complexity of the action, barely hinted at in the brief plot summaries above, the Lensmen saga does possess the unity described at the beginning of this chapter; Smith planned very carefully what he wanted to do, and he employed all his intelligence and his developing skill in doing it. This point should emerge clearly from a discussion of what actually is going on in the novels. By exploring some major aspects of the Lensmen books, I hope to show how Smith worked around his weaknesses as a writer and exploited his strengths.

One thing that may strike a modern science-fiction reader as a weakness of the Lensmen novels is the overall lack of social extrapolation: What changes occur in attitudes and institutions as a result of the Lens' presence? Smith's forte is technological extrapolation, showing how one device leads the way to another; the society surrounding the weapons' systems is rather hazy. That was true of the Skylark novels too, but it is even more obvious here. In the Civilization of the far future, people conduct business about the same as they do now, they use much the same slang, they entertain themselves in identical ways--they even write and read pulp science-fiction adventures.

One area of haziness is especially disturbing. Politics is seldom mentioned in the Lensmen novels. In First Lensman, while running for President of North America, Rod Kinnison suggests that all power should be in the hands of Lensmen, who by definition are trustworthy and who can prove their honesty telepathically at any time. In the later novels, it appears that this transfer has taken place, so there is no longer any need for politics as we know it. This fits with Smith's general distrust of the mass of humanity, shown most strongly in First Lensman. On one hand, Virgil Samms and his Lensmen believe that if the people are shown the truth, they will naturally side with the Lensmen (p. 190; p. 157); on the other hand, however, as the election draws closer, the voters remain undecided.

They might have seen the truth, Smith bitterly comments, "If they had cared enough about the basic issues involved to make the necessary mental effort, but almost everyone was too busy doing something else. And it was so much easier to take somebody else's word for it. And finally, thinking is an exercise to which all too few brains are accustomed" (p. 296; p. 243). The right side barely wins the election. And the glimpses of people outside the Patrol, in the later novels, do not suggest that they are much more responsible than those who encumbered the early stages of Civilization.

It appears that Smith was not much interested in describing changes to society because he was not much interested in how the masses of humanity tottered about. In the epilogue to the magazine version of Skylark Three, remember, Smith suggested the outline of a galactic Civilization, but he did not use subsequent Skylark novels to fill in that outline, instead reverting to the Seaton-DuQuesne era. In much the same way, he leaves the nature of Civilization—whatever it does when not fighting Boskone—extremely vague in the Lensmen novels. This is especially apparent when Smith tries to suggest a contrast between Boskone's populated planets and Civilization's, suggesting why and how a culture could be converted from Boskone to Civilization. Generally, however, Smith's lack of detail in presenting Civilization is not a serious problem, since the readers has little time to worry about whatever society might be supposed to exist as background for the action. Moreover, Smith's lack of interest in the masses of society is balanced by his very strong interest in the individual, acting and growing apart from society.

Yet some people consider characterization to be a major weakness in Smith's fiction. Critics generally dismiss space opera, in which they usually toss Smith's work, as concentrating on action at the expense of character; to accommodate themselves to the breakneck pace of the action, the characters tend to be flat stereotypes.

In fact, a number of Smith's characters are striking and memorable. Minor characters, such as Surgeon-Marshall Lacy, Port Admiral Haynes, and Peter Van Buskirk, stand up well. Though, like many of Charles Dickens' characters, they are constructed as the embodiment of one personality trait, they do embody that trait vividly. Smith's alien characters are memorable, too. From the boisterous Worsel to the lower-than-low-key Nadreck, they have enough human traits to be related to, but enough strangeness to show that they are other than human.

It is true, however, that Smith at first seems less convincing when he tries to show a major character in much

depth. Perhaps, literally, the major characters in the
Lensmen novels have little depth. Smith's characters tend
to be immediately, spontaneously good—or capable of switch-
ing allegiance to good very easily—or utterly evil. Very
few show the ambivalent mixture of good and evil traits we
are used to seeing in modern fiction and have been convinced
we should recognize in ourselves. If Kim, Chris, and their
children have no human weaknesses, how can a reader feel
that they are human? Without convincing human characters,
how can a story give more than a flash of exciting action?
Kim's rebellious outburst at the beginning of Second Stage
Lenmen is, after all, soon overcome and it is balanced at
the novel's end by his checking with Mentor of Arisia for
permission to go ahead and marry Chris. Even the novel that
contains most expressions of emotion, Children of the Lens,
may be read by jaded readers as a put-up job, Kim and Chris
proclaiming the emotions they are supposed to feel because
of their heroic roles rather than being forced to reveal
their human feelings. They speak emotional lines, but with
a hint of too-perfect posturing. In much the same way, even
when Kim must absorb drugs and liquor so he can play the
part of asteroid miner Wild Bill Williams in Gray Lensman,
he naturally loathes them (it helps that he can keep his
Lensman's consciousness awake even while his body is
paralyzed), and he never becomes addicted. When, after the
imposture is over, Haynes queries him, Kim replies: "'Some
craving, of course . . . . That can't be helped—you can't
make an omelette without breaking eggs. However, it's nothing I can't lick. I've got it pretty well boiled out of my
system already'" (p. 173; p. 146). That is the end of it.
Such steadiness is alien to most human experience. A modern
reader may feel that without characters capable of feeling,
real, lasting conflict or temptation there can be no genuine
internal struggle—and no exultation in overcoming these internal demons. From such a viewpoint, the Lensmen novels
would be inherently limited, simple-minded entertainments.

But such a dismissal is not fair. After all, the
Lensmen are the best of Civilization. They are naturally
able, and they have been tested to verify their absolute
trustworthiness, their freedom from disabling inner
division. That much is spelled out at the beginning of
Galactic Patrol, when Commandant of Cadets Fritz von Hohen-
dorff describes how the five years of training for the
Galactic Patrol reduce the one million in the first year
class to one hundred by graduation. Moreover, Kim and Chris
are the product of the Arisians' breeding program to produce
the parents of the next stage of human development; they are
the embodiments of the strongest, finest traits imaginable.

By definition, they must show their superior natures.

It is difficult for a writer to show a truly superior human being's nature without making him seen a _less_ than "human" character. Without blasphemy, we may recall that Jesus at least portrays human selfishness in His prayer that the cup of suffering pass from Him and at least mimes despair in the cry, "'My God, my God, why hast thou forsaken me!'" Such flashes of feeling help make Him a person with whom one can identify and believe in. If Kim is too perfect to show such traits, however, we must remember that he does not have Jesus' advantage of direct contact with a diety. In fact, Kim does not have the luxury of appealing to anyone or anything outside himself. He is the one in charge, and he must find the strength within himself to accomplish what must be done.(4) In Children of the Lens, the Children do show convincing anguish at the discovery they are superhuman and thus cut off from the rest of humanity. But they also get themselves under control soon. They must. They have their job to do, and they must do it themselves. Though the Arisians actually are almost omniscient and seem close to omnipotent, they are very careful about intervening directly in human affairs, preferring to let Kim and the others stand (or fall) by themselves.

If the main characters of the Lensmen novels can be understood as naturally superior people who know they must _use_ their superiority all the time, this gives special force to Mentor of Arisia's constant demand: Think! If the characters have little need to develop emotionally, they have immense need to develop cognitively. Their difficulties convince them that they must increase the range and flexibility of their thinking; this leads them to realize that no one's mind is capable of doing everything that must be done; this, in turn, leads to contact with alien minds and specialized abilities. The highest achievement of individual thinking, shown in the whole Lensmen corps and capped by the Children's fusion into their Unit for special tasks, is the ability to appreciate and coordinate _different_ attitudes. It may be paradoxical that Smith actually sets up that difference within a rather narrow band of character traits displayed by the characters he likes; nevertheless, the employment of Dickensian exaggeration of personality traits to label a cast of supporting characters does create enough sense of individual difference to make this aspect of Smith's overall intention clear and acceptable, too.

Actually, one of the great strengths of the Lensmen saga--something quite unexpected considering the loose improvisation of the Skylark series--is how neatly the series is structured: enough action to keep readers busy and enough bulk to mask purely didactic lecturing, while concepts are expanded by the experience of individuals.

At that, the Lensmen novels utilize a trait already seen in the Skylark series: each major development is merely preparation for the next mental leap. Now, however, Smith exploits this quality by ending each of the magazine Lensmen novels with a climax that finishes everything a reader is likely to imagine—then beginning the next novel with the revelation that there is _more_. This is a striking enough experience for readers who have all the novels waiting in a neat pile and who know exactly how many books remain unread in the series; it was much more striking for Smith's original readers, who saw each novel serialized in Astounding, read the last installment, and naturally enough let the Lensmen saga settle comfortably in their minds, content the story was over. James H. Schmitz, for example, describes his reaction to the conclusion of Gray Lensman and the beginning of the next novel:

> I watched the Gray Lensman walk away, hand in hand with Clarissa MacDougall, that magnificent auburn-haired nurse of the Patrol, into a well-earned, blissful future. "Good-bye and good luck, old pal!" I lensed sentimentally after him. "It's been rare fun knocking around the galaxies with you . . ."
> About two years later on my time—though only some thirty seconds later on Kinnison's—the Historian of the Boskonian War lowered the boom on the Gray Lensman's prospects for an immediate carefree future. Part One of a new serial appeared in Astounding Science Fiction. Its title: "Second Stage Lensmen." And it began:
> "Stop, youth!" The voice of Mentor the Arisian thundered silently, deep within the Lensman's brain.
> Kinnison, and I, stopped convulsively, almost in mid-stride—and at the rigid, absent awareness in our eyes, Nurse MacDougall's beautiful face went white. . . (5)

It is not unusual for a piece of popular fiction to build excitement by creating crises that break off in cliff-hanger chapter endings. Smith certainly knew how to do that. He also knew, and did skillfully in the Lensmen novels, how to end a whole novel with a conclusion that actually is a disguised cliff-hanger.

The effect of this is to demonstrate for the Lensmen

and for the readers that there is no real end to an action, only a constant process of growth. As far as mind-stretching "sense of wonder," Smith's description of colliding planets at the end of Gray Lensman is as fine as anything he ever did. But that is only one stage in the development of weapons. Rather than dwelling on that effect, Smith leaps to the next concept. Everything in the Lensmen novels—humans groping for understanding, recognizing their own weakness, seeking help from beings they might instinctively reject as monstrous, recognizing the importance of respecting and balancing differences, etc.—is reintroduced from novel to novel in different aspects, always more complex, more challenging. Smith's structuring of the novels introduces readers to these themes in manageable portions but keeps soaring through the exploration of new ideas, new wonders.

Looking at the aspects of the Lensmen novels discussed here, one may ask: What is the reason for such an unsettling structure? Why is it important that characters keep themselves under control so they can do their duties? What is the nature of Civilization? If these ultimately seem workable facets of the Lensmen novels, what is the work Smith is using them to do? Quite a bit, actually; he has an overwhelmingly important concern that rouses all his writing skills to make the Lensmen novels even more than the apotheosis of science-fiction adventure. Smith is trying to settle something that kept getting out of control in the Skylark books: He wants to show the difference between Good and Evil. Moreover, he wants to show why the difference matters and how readers can make their choices count.

As the earlier plot summary has indicated, the Arisians represent Good, the Eddorians Evil. In depicting Evil, Smith is fairly effective in demonstrating the sadism of the Overlords of Delagon. However, the novels exhibit less overt sexual depravity, very little of the drunken or drug-crazed behavior that sometimes passes for Evil in fiction. Smith avoided this kind of surface description because of the publishing restrictions of the time and because of his own taste. He also perceived Evil at another, deeper level, though. For Smith, the root of Evil is unthinking, unrestrained exercise of selfishness, ego, in the exercise of power. Thus, the constant, petty rudeness that all minions of Boskone show each other is a natural, believable expression of their selfishness. If this unvarying rudeness seems unbelievably impractical, readers should check accounts of Hitler's Germany and Stalin's Kremlin. They also should review the transcripts of tapes from the Nixon White House. As George Orwell speculated in 1984, the true purpose of power in a totalitarian society is the exercise of power itself, while personal relations sink below the level of barbarism.

Good, on the other hand, is shown in the Lensmen series as recognition of diversity, especially racial and sexual differences. Good accepts the independence of other beings, permitting them room to think and grow on their own. As the Arisians explain, fruitlessly, to Helmuth when he tries to reach their planet, "'liberty--of person, of thought, of action--is the basic and the goal of the civilization to which you are opposed, and with which any really philosophical mind must find itself in accord'" (GP, p. 135; p. 121).

If Smith is right, and if he can create a structure and characters to show it, he can use the Lensmen novels to show how the natural power of Good will overcome Evil through the process of transforming "Civilization."

To see what Smith is working toward, let us compare the Lensmen novels to the work of another early twentieth-century writer: Jack London. Smith and London are strongly similar in several ways. Both were "popular" writers, difficult for academic critics to appreciate initially. Both considered themselves primarily storytellers, writing slangy but vigorous prose. And both men dealt with similar concerns. Both watched the rise and clash of alien cultures and wondered: On what basis does one society rise and another fall? Both, living in a West that had not emotionally acknowledged the closing of the American frontier, saw collective society absorbing the individual and wondered: What is the relation between individual and mass? Finally, both were aware of the increased, mind-numbing standardization of life around them and wondered: How can a superior individual survive and use his gifts?

Both London and Smith were concerned with the dramatically superior individual, the "superman." Both assumed that the true superman would be essentially altruistic and would use his intelligence to see dangers to the common good that the ordinary person could not perceive. But both also feared that warnings might only disturb the unseeing mob. Certainly the superman would be opposed by non-altruistic people who feared progress; such people might be inferior to the superman in natural ability, but they could ally themselves with general craving for comfort and untroubled stasis.

Smith and London differ, however, in the solutions they see for this conflict. London offers a political answer that is less plausible the more one considers it. Smith concentrates on demonstrating a change in outlook that might be more difficult to put into effect than London's proposal-

--but that might more directly deal with the problem of the superman's uneasy role.

London believed in a world composed only of natural, physical forces. He believed that superior traits sometimes appeared in individuals and that through natural selection those traits could pass from one generation to another, reshaping the race. This picture of evolution is singularly discomforting, however. London was too realistic to imagine that the superior individual would be superior enough to see apart from the perspective his social context offered him. Therefore, he was bound to make dreadful mistakes, lose opportunities, and quite possibly fail ultimately. In Before Adam (1906), one of London's stories of prehistoric man, perspective is supplied by a modern man who is conscious of the racial memories of a distant ancestor. Looking back, unable to change any of the past events, the narrator comments again and again on how much was wasted. The primitive man domesticates a dog, navigates a rudimentary raft, etc., but profits by none of these discoveries. He is a creature of his time; he cannot grasp the possibilities of his innovations. He is limited by the brute side of humanity, both figuratively by his own vagaries and literally by the presence of Red-Eye, the atavism, who constantly disrupts the social arrangements of the tribe and kills anyone who interferes with him. The narrator can look back in time, down at primitive man, and regret the missed opportunities. The early man can only live, pushed about by circumstances. And the last thing the narrator sees, after his ancestors' branch of the tribe has been destroyed, is Red-Eye, comfortable and feared in a tribe he can dominate.

London's narrator stresses how these primitive humans show the basis for our more refined feelings of friendship and love. The reverse is true also, unfortunately. Man still feels the power of the ativistic, brute drives that will disrupt every settled arrangement. In addition, the superior human being is limited by his time; there are important things that he simply cannot see. And even if he tries to raise his head out of the well-worn rut, he cannot act effectively to prevent disaster.

In London's novel The Iron Heel (1907), for example, Ernest Everhard is markedly superior to the people around him, quite possibly a superman. He is intelligent enough to realize, eventually, that the power of the workers he is attempting to rouse to action is less than that of the capitalists. He foresees very accurately the rise of the Oligarchy, driving the masses into slavery. He even understands that his own efforts may bring the emergence of the brutal power even sooner. Still he continues working, for

52

he believes that eventually a socialist state will replace the fascist Iron Heel. The novel proclaims that he is right in this prophecy also. Still, a reader's satisfaction at this conclusion is somewhat muted. Everhard's vision for the race is an ultimate success, but an immediate failure. Capitalism butchers countless workers to establish the Oligarchy and destroys countless more while it lasts. Even with a more conscious superman than in Before Adam, The Iron Heel still offers a picture of humanity stumbling forward, unable to avoid much misery along its path. Though the race progresses, the superior individual does not live to see the success. He is out of place, and he is destroyed in the upheaval he has helped create.

Even the progress of the race is less than completely convincing to a reader. Everhard's story is presented through a manuscript discovered centuries later; the introduction and footnotes insist that a socialist state has replaced the Oligarchy. However, the action of the story itself moves toward dissolution and retreat, breaking off in mid-sentence. The glorious new world remains somehow tenuous and abstract. Suspicion of the optimistic conclusion's solidity is reinforced by a look at London's other books, which also show the superior individual out of place in a mediocre world. He may lie to himself to escape his need to excel (as in Burning Daylight) or he may simply die (as in The Sea Wolf); the fact remains that there is no place where he can freely develop and use his powers.

London's optimism is essentially a product of the will, not the imagination. London believes that we all are trapped by natural law, inferior and superior alike. He believes there is no way to escape this trap. Even though he wants to believe some alteration of the political system would free the superman's abilities, he is unable to show this actually happening. No doubt part of his having a higher reputation than Smith is due to his work being more "realistic" in setting and in its emphasis on human failure and on the power of blind chance in human life. But actually Smith offers more than escape from a world dominated by failure and chance. Rather, he presents an alternative based on reforming, reshaping, of individual consciousness. Smith deserves respect for making a serious attempt to imagine how a superior individual might be able to survive and thrive—and how others could reflect the role of superman in themselves.

At first glance, the superior individual seems as much an outsider in Smith's Civilization as he does in London's world. Triplanetary, remember, begins with a description of the cyclic rise and fall of civilizations. In each cycle,

Smith shows a superior human being failing, and with him, the civilization and the race itself is defeated. The section closest to our own times shows Ralph Kinnison's struggle against greed and bureaucratic incompetence during World War II. Like the other superior people Smith shows in this part of the book, Kinnison demonstrates his own superiority but does not prevail. Although he maintains his principles and leaves the scene with his head high, the villains keep their position and prestige. In any event, not many years later, one of Kinnison's descendants is vaporized while defending America from the atomic attack that begins World War III.

Despite this rather grim beginning, Smith's attitude is fundamentally different than London's. Smith does not believe that humanity is the product of blind evolution, and he does not believe that humanity succeeds or fails purely by chance. He pictures intelligence directing the forces that work for evil or good in human life: Eddore and Arisia, respectively. Thus, Eddore is responsible for the collapse of each civilization, while Arisia helps humanity climb back to a higher level.

The important thing to remember, however, is that (for different reasons) these forces do not direct every action: not all good comes from Arisia, nor all evil from Eddore. The shoddiness and treachery Ralph Kinnison encounters during World War II, for example, is purely human villainy. In fact, Smith is concerned with a different level of life. London believes that an individual who tries to succeed alone is doomed, because the possibilities of human life are determined by the natural world, especially its economics. Smith believes that it is the scope and direction of the individual consciousness that determines the possibilities of human life. He also believes that the development of the individual and the group are intimately related; one makes the other possible. Therefore, we must see how Eddore and Arisia correspond to directions of human desires, asking what these directions represent and what possibilities for human growth they show.

Eddore is based on thorough understanding of physical force, but it finds no satisfaction in knowledge. Rather, the hallmark of Eddore is hunger for power over things and over other beings, especially the sweet, protracted imposition of one's own will on another intelligence. Acting through several layers of the organization called Boskone, it tries to subvert and destroy Civilization, which only belatedly realizes that it is dealing with an organized entity rather than a swarm of pirates. In fact, organization is an integral aspect of Eddore-Boskone, as shown in an early meeting of Eddore's innermost circle that dictates:

"We must work through echelon upon echelon of
higher and lower executives and supervisors if
we are to control effectively the activities of
the thousands of billions of operators which we
must and will have at work" (T, p. 252; p. 212).

In the scene as a whole, however, the Eddorians do not
merely make the plans but gloat over them. The prospect of
"control" is a goal in itself for the Eddorians. What they
rationalize as an impersonally efficient system is actually
a device by which a being at a superior level can shield
himself while belittling and manipulating those beneath him.
At a much more brutal level, apparently unconnected with Eddore at first, are the Overlords of Delgon, who mentally
control victims whom they lure to caverns, then torture to
death while feeding on their life force. Later in the
story, the Overlords become allies of Boskone—an altogether
natural partnership since the Overlords do more thoroughly
what the others do figuratively every day in their personal
dealings. All Eddore-Boskone is characterized by basic
selfishness and a willingness for—even a delight in—
tormenting and crushing someone else.

Such an attitude creates severe drawbacks for the Eddorian organization. For one thing, real morale is lacking.
For another, there is little imagination, because every part
of the organization is controlled by some other part while
it nervously-avidly maintains control over its area of
responsibility. In combat, the spacefleets of Boskone
repeatedly are defeated by Civilization because they cannot
improvise; if the chain of command is broken, the lower elements do not know what to do. If they make a mistake, they
will be punished; even if they are successful without
orders, they will be punished. Consequently, they hesitate,
fumble, and die.

But the most basic weakness of Eddore-Boskone is the
lack of imagination at the highest levels of the operation.
It is altogether natural to see another in terms of oneself.
Even Civilization, as noted above, is slow to realize that
Boskone is an elaborate organization rather than a loose
federation of individuals. However, Civilization is able to
recognize its mistake and alter its tactics. Eddore remains
hopelessly confused because it sees Civilization in terms of
itself and is utterly unable to learn otherwise. Rather
than understanding that they are threatened by a loose association of Lensmen under the leadership of Kimball
Kinnison, the Eddorians are convinced that there must be one

master Lensman:

> Lensmen, hundreds of them, each worked upon
> definite assignment. None of them had ever seen
> or ever would see the man who issued orders . .
> . . They received orders through their Lenses,
> wherever they might be in space. They reported
> back to him in the same way (GL, p. 245; p.
> 204).

This is, of course, exactly how Boskone itself is organized.
It seems reassuringly natural to the Eddorians that they
enemies would follow the same pattern. Consequently, they
spend their time and energy pursuing the mythical master
Lensman, "Star A Star," while Kinnison and his cohorts chip
away at their rigid structure. Occasionally, as when the
members of Boskone debate the nature of Star A Star in the
sixteenth chapter of Second Stage Lensmen, they wander
perilously close to the truth. But they cannot grasp it.
Their whole world view makes it impossible for them to imagine an active group that is at once effective and
decentralized, combining for a common purpose and operating
together when necessary without stratifying and degrading
its component parts.

Eddore is, in effect, doomed by the fierce, greedy independence that actually subverts its apparently-facile
organization. That "organization" keeps the members from
ever truly cooperating. Even at the climax of Children of
the Lens, with annihilation imminent, the Eddorians are unable to go beyond that attitude. One of the planet's
defenders appeals to His Ultimate Supremacy for aid:

> "My message is this: solve for us, and quickly,
> the problem of this attacking unity. If you do
> not or cannot do so, we perish all of us, even
> to you of the Innermost Circle."
> "Think you so?" The thought was a sneer. "If
> your fusions cannot match those of the Arisians
> you should die, and the loss will be small" (CL,
> p. 278; pp. 240-241).

To be allied with Eddore, to reflect Eddorian values,
is to be trapped within one's nature and controlled by the
direction of that nature. On the other hand, Arisia represents not physical but mental power, not control but desire
for growth and recognition that personal growth must be ac-
companied by growth of the people around one. Rather than
the rigid hierarchy of Boskone, Civilization encourages

greater and greater freedom for its members, culminating in the Release that gives a Lensman the right to do practically anything at all he wishes. This might appear to be much more dangerous than Boskone's rigid control over the individual. The results prove otherwise. Not only are the Lensmen carefully selected by trained and prepared for freedom. They discover, without much fuss, that they are ready simply to do what must be done, not waste time in bullying others. Besides, there is pleasure in working for more than oneself; Kim converts one agent of Boskone by asking whether altruism or selfishness would be more "fun" (SSL, p. 291; p. 256). Being an ally of Arisia, reflecting Arisian values, means trying to satisfy an urge to share rather than dominate, admitting that one can gain more from others by meeting them as partners than by demanding their submission.

Smith's Civilization is based on respect for the individual, as an individual and as a possible member of an intimate group. The first book in the series, Triplanetary, faces the issue of xenophobia squarely, when aliens examine human victims and conclude that "'by no stretch of the imagination can they be compared to us. I am quite relieved-- I was afraid that in my haste I might have slain members of a highly developed race'" (pp. 154-155; p. 135). The human response, immediately following, mirrors this attitude. Later, the humans gain respect for the aliens as "'big and . . . clean'" (p. 270; p. 226)--especially in contrast to the agents of Eddore operating in the novel--and humans and aliens are able to communicate and bring their conflict to a reasonable conclusion. This attitude is carried much farther in later Lensmen novels. Smith shows repeatedly that any type of intelligent being whatsoever may be Lensman material and thus worthy of trust and admiration. It follows that any human at all is worthy of respect as a possible companion.

Smith also shows respect for the individual but emphasis on cooperation in describing the relation of the sexes. In many ways, the Lensmen novels seem to picture women in a traditional, stereotyped role. In other ways, women behave very surprisingly. In fact, Smith did believe that men and women had different roles in life, for he believed that they were fundamentally different types of person. This made the union of man and woman even more important to Smith, because the ability to relate to free, unique individuals was so important to him. The flaw of the Matriarchy on Lyrane II is not that women have taken man's place but that they admit no place in their society for men. Kim finds them appalling

to any really human being, whose entire outlook
and existence is fundamentally, however uncon-
sciously or subconsciously, based up and conditioned by the prime division of life into two
cooperant sexes . . . . In cold reality, these
women were no more human than were the . . .
Eich. Take the Posenians, or the Rigellians, or
even the Valantians. Any normal, stay-at-home
Tellurian woman would pass out cold if she happened to stumble onto Worsel in a dark alley at
night. Yet members of his repulsively
reptilian-appearing race, merely because of
having a heredity of equality and cooperation
between sexes, were in essence more nearly human
than were these tall, splendidly-built, actually
and intrinsically beautiful creatures of Lyrane
II! (SSL, p. 61; pp. 58-59).

In even more extreme fashion, the fact that the Eddorians
are absolutely sexless and have an affinity for sexless
races (CL, pp. 208-209; pp. 182-183) again demonstrates the
Eddorian inability to share in any way with another being.
    The power of these relationships--Civilization,
Lensmen, sexual--is shown at the end of the series as the
Children of the Lens destroy Eddore. It is shown again,
even more clearly, as Clarissa Kinnison and her superhuman
children reach beyond themselves, beyond even the range of
Arisian understanding, to rescue Kim Kinnison from the
stasis in which he is sealed. Although male Lensmen are
supposed to be the ones with the strongest personal "drive,"
it is Chris whose frenzied love gives the Unit power to do
what the Arisians believe cannot be done. Love is literally
beyond comprehension, even for the Arisians (CL, p. 287; p.
248); all they can do is approvingly recognize that it
exists, creating something more than the sum of its parts.
    Thus the Arisian way of internal growth, sympathetic
mind vs. physical force, ultimately is vindicated by the
Lensmen novels. The characters are free to grow mentally
and emotionally, despite their physical circumstances. The
root of the growth, however, is respect for the separateness
of individuals. The ideal relationship is between equals,
but one cannot count on this. When unequal parties come
together, it is up to the superior individual to make sure
that the relationship is like that of parent and child,
teacher and student. The other must be nurtured, not
smothered. Above all, the superior individual must avoid
displaying superiority when it would simply encourage the

other to develop an inferiority complex (CL, p. 6; p. 11);
the child-student must be allowed to handle things alone
(CL, p. 79, 102; p. 74, 94). For even the superior individual recognizes that growth comes from recognizing
weaknesses and trying to stretch past them.

All this is demonstrated in the climax of the Lensmen
saga, in which the children must protect and nurture their
parents. As they do maintain that relationship of respect
and love for their less superhuman father and mother, the
Children of the Lens become conscious of their own immense
superiority to everyone around them. They are frightened,
dismayed to think of being unique and alone (CL, pp. 87-88;
pp. 81-82). But they ultimately are reassured. Before
leaving them as Guardians of Civilization, Mentor of Arisia
tells them that "all shall be well" (CL, p. 292; p. 253);
much earlier, their father had experienced a moment of doubt
as he contemplated the vastness of space, then pulled himself together:

> He got up, shaking off the futile mood. . . .
> he had a job to do. And after all, wasn't man
> as big as space? Could he have come out here,
> otherwise? He was. Yes, man was bigger even
> than space. Man, by his very envisionment of
> macro-cosmic space, had already mastered it (GL,
> p. 48; p. 45).

The result of personal growth along with respect for
the individuality of others is self-confidence. After all,
growth is a natural part of life; it is proper and fitting
that individuals and races change. Especially in the vast
time the Children of the Lens can expect to live, they certainly can grow by themselves and find others to relate to
as equals. They already have learned, by example and by
their own experience, tolerance for all manner of
differences, rather than a haughty attitude that considers
difference as inferiority. They have been able to come to
recognize their own flaws and limitations. From all this
comes respect, for others and themselves. And from this
comes love.

Through the Lensmen novels, Smith leads readers to see
and share these values. By doing so, along with showing the
planet-hurling, galaxy-spanning action, he tries to stretch
readers' minds. His last words are aimed directly at the
reader: you are a potential superman, too, or you could not
have received this message in the first place. Kit
Kinnison's words end the saga: "One of us will become en
rapport with you as soon as you have assimilated the facts,

59

the connotations, and the implications of this material. Prepare your mind for contact" (CL, p. 293; p. 255).

This involvement of the reader in the moral struggle for contact/growth is the result of Smith's careful preparation. His apparent neglect of social or economic extrapolation actually lets him focus on the role of the individual. His seeming failure to depict characters floundering in turmoil actually lets him concentrate on characters who are ready for immense personal growth (from, admittedly, an unusually strong foundation). The structure of the novels reinforces his concerns, a well-tempered humanism. It is an impressive achievement. All things considered, the Lensmen novels do deserve the label "masterpiece" that many of Smith's fans have given them.

NOTES

(1)   Smith's essay "The Epic of Space" appeared in Of Worlds Beyond: The Science of Science Fiction Writing (Reading, PA: Fantasy Press, 1947; rpt. Chicago: Advent, 1964), pp. 77-87. Hereafter cited in text.

(2)   In fact, Smith wrote the climax of Children of the Lens "before the final draft of 'Galactic Patrol' was mailed to Astounding" (letter to Alva Rogers, quoted in Rogers' A Requiem for Astounding (Chicago: Advent, 1964), pp. 152-153, planning everything in the novels to build to that conclusion.

(3)   Women cannot be Lensmen, it is announced, because they lack the intense drive that men possess (FL, p. 42; p. 38). That statement is debatable, as will be seen later; it represents the best understanding that Civilization is capable of at the moment, no more.

(4)   Formal religion barely appears at all in the Lensmen novels. In fact, the spacemen have created their own god, Klono, as the focus of various oaths so they can blow off steam; there is no hint that they actually worship Klono.

(5)   "Introduction" to Ron Ellik and Bill Evans, The Universes of E. E. Smith (Chicago: Advent, 1966), p. 8.

VI

OTHER WRITING

Smith's reputation rightly is based on his two major
series. However, the remainder of Smith's fiction deserves
some attention too, for it contains some surprising excel-
lences and some fascinating insights into Smith's thinking.

Revisions
     As might be expected from Smith's approach to
composition, especially as described in the chapter on the
Skylark series, he never regarded a piece of fiction as
quite finished. This can be seen by the way he went through
his novels before letting them be republished. Part of the
revision of the Lensmen novels consisted of spelling out the
terms of the underlying conflict. In the magazine version
of Second Stage Lensmen, for example, Kim's struggle with
Fossten-Gharlane is described as follows:

> Indomitably, relentlessly, the Gray
> Lensman held his offense upon that unimaginably
> high level; his Lens flooding the room with in-
> tensely coruscant poly-chromatic light. He did
> not know, then or ever, how he did it. It
> seemed as though his lens, of its own volition
> in this time of ultimate need, reached out into
> unguessable continua and drew therefrom an
> added, an extra something (Astounding, February
> 1942, p. 110).

By the addition of a new sentence, the book version reveals
something only hinted at in the second and third sentences
of the first version:

> Indomitably, relentlessly, the Gray Lensman
> held his offense upon that unimaginably high
> level; his Lens flooding the room with intensely
> coruscant polychromatic light. He did not know
> [emphasis added], then or ever, how he did it.
> He never did suspect that he was not alone. It
> seemed [emphasis added] as though his Lens, of
> its own volition in this time of ultimate need,
> reach out into unguessable continua and drew
> therefrom an added, an extra something (SSL, p.
> 269; p. 237).

No other words in the passage are changed. As I argued in the previous chapter, the heroism of lesser characters is not diminished when they receive aid from their superiors. Still, the superior Arisians never reveal to Kim that they boosted his strength so he could overcome Gharlane, and the readers of the Lensmen novels as first published were also kept in the dark. Such additions were necessary throughout the complete Lensmen saga to show how the action constantly related to the Arisia-Eddore conflict.

Smith also did more complex revisions, sometimes subtly altering the focus of scenes. Consider the scene in Second Stage Lensmen in which Clarissa, Kim, and the other male Second Stage Lensmen determine that a nest of the Overlords has been established on Lyrane II. First, Chris presents the information she has gathered about mysterious disappearances. The book version omits a timid sentence from the end of her listing of facts: "'I'm sorry that I couldn't get any real information; that this jumble is all I could discover for you'" (Astounding, December 1941, p. 54). The next paragraph describes the grouping of marks on a map to record disappearances; again, however, the last sentence of the paragraph is omitted from the book version: "To four of the Lensmen present [the males] the full grisly meaning of the thing was starkly plain." Next, Smith's revision adds a paragraph describing Chris drawing the evidence together, though she is not self-confident enough to state the conclusion:

> "Almost all the lines intersect at this point here," she went on, placing a finger-tip near the north pole of the globe. . . . If it is Overlords, their cavern must be within about fifty kilometers of the spot I've marked here. However, I couldn't find any evidence that any Eich have ever been here; and if they haven't I don't see how the Overlords could be here, either. That, gentlemen of the Second Stage, is my report; which, I fear, is neither complete nor conclusive" (SSL, p. 159; p. 143).

The other's response has also been subtly altered. In the magazine version, the next paragraph reads as follows: "Nadreck was the first to speak. 'Ah, very well done, Lensman MacDougall,' he congratulated. 'Your data are amply sufficient. A right scholarly and highly informative bit of work, eh, friend Worsel?'" The book version differs: "'You err, Lensman MacDougall.' Nadreck was the first to speak.

'It is both [complete and conclusive]. A right scholarly and highly informative piece of work, eh, friend Worsel?'"

In the revised scene, Smith strengthens the role of Chris, downplaying her hesitancy and letting the solution come from her, rather than from the male Lensmen who must pull together the data she merely has gathered.

A final thing that shows up in Smith's revisions is his effort to make his writing more direct by streamlining and condensing it. In the scene's final passages, besides reducing the stereotyping of Chris's role, revisions definitely tighten the wording. The Lensmen still are discussing the discovery of the Overlord nest. In the magazine version, the scene continues as Kim speaks:

"If I had [know Overlords were operating near his beloved], I'd've had a hundred Lyranians mob you, Chris, and tie you down. It would be just about here, I'd say, from the trend of the lines of vanishment." He placed a finger-tip near the north pole of the globe. He thought for a moment, his jaw setting and his eyes growing hard, then spoke aloud to the girl. "Chris, the next time I tell you to hide and you don't do it I'm going to take that Lens away from you and flash it with a DeLameter—then you'll go back to Tellus and you'll stay there." His voice was grimmer than she had ever before heard it.

"You don't mean . . . why it can't be . . . you're all thinking . . . Overlords!" she gasped. Her face turned white; both hands flew to her throat.

"Just that. Overlords. Nothing else but." He pictured in imagination his fiancee's body writhing in torment from a Delgonian torture screen until his mind revolted; all unconscious that his thoughts were as clear as a telescreen picture to all the others. "If they had detected you—You know that they would do anything to get hold of a mind and a vital force like yours—but, thank all the gods of space, they didn't." He shook himself and drew a tremendously deep breath of relief. "Well, all I've got to say is that if we ever have any kids and they don't bawl when I tell them about this I'll certainly give them something to bawl about!"

"But listen, Kim!" Clarissa protested. "What makes you all so sure that it's Overlords? There's nothing on my map there to prove--why, it might be <u>anything</u>!"

"It might not, too," Kinnison stated. "Barring the contingency of the existence of a life form unknown to any of the four of us and which operates exactly as the Overlords do operate, that hypothesis is the only one both necessary and sufficient to explain all the facts which you have plotted upon your chart. Think a minute--you know how they work. They tune in on some one mind, the stronger and more vital the better. The fact that the Lyranians have such powerful minds is undoubtedly one big reason why the Overlords are here. In that connection, it's a mystery to me how Helen, ruler of the Lyranians, has lived so long--all the persons who disappeared had high-powered minds, didn't they?"

She thought for a space. "Now that you mention it, I believe that they did; as far as I know anyway" (<u>Astounding</u>, December 1941, p. 54; January 1942, p. 98).

Now the book version:

"If I had, you'd never've got that Lens, Clarissa May MacDougall." His voice was the grimmest she had ever heard it. He was picturing to himself her lovely body writhing in torment; stretched, twisted, broken; forgetting completely that his thoughts were as clear as a tri-di to all the others.

"If they had detected <u>you</u> . . . you know what they'd do to get hold of a mind and a vital force such as yours. . ."

He shook himself and drew a tremendously deep breath of relief. "But thank God they didn't. So all I've got to say is that if we ever have any kids and they don't bawl when I tell 'em about this, I'll certainly give 'em something to bawl about!"

"But listen, Kim!" Clarissa protested. "All four of you are assuming that I've dead-centered the target. I thought probably I was right, but since I couldn't find any Eich traces, I expected a lot of argument."

"No argument," Kinnison assured her. "You know how they work. They tune in on some one mind, the stronger and more vital the better. In that connection, I wonder that Helen is still around--the ones who disappeared were upper-bracket minds, weren't they?"

She thought a space. "Now that you mention it, I believe so. Most of them, certainly" (SSL, pp. 160-161; pp. 143-144).

Even these samples should show that Smith's revisions were extensive and painstaking. He never boasted about the quality of his writing, replying to one young critic that "he wrote as well as he could and could continue to do his best to satisfy his audience."(1) He considered himself an unpretentious storyteller, striving for efficiency in the telling of his stories. But he became more efficient as he went along, polishing and smoothing his writing at least into the 1960s, to lessen the gap between descriptions of stunning catastrophes (such as the climax of Gray Lensman) that seize a reader's full attention, and more mundane actions and conversations that seem banal by comparison.

Non-Series Novels
Spacehounds of IPC was first published as a three-part serial in Amazing, beginning in the July 1931 issue. At the time, Smith believed that he had closed off the Skylark series, and he planned the new novel as the first of a new series. It remains a false start for several reasons. For one, Smith was irritated by changes that editor T. O'Conor Sloane made in the published text and decided to shift his writing to other magazines.(2) Also, Smith was upset when readers were less enthusiastic about Spacehounds than they had been about the Skylark stories; he had taken pains not to indulge in the violations of probability that had bothered a few readers of the Skylark novels, this time restricting himself to the boundaries of the solar system. Readers--and editor Sloane, too--wistfully suggested that he should let his imagination run free in the future.
In any event, Spacehounds of IPC is a fast-moving, ef-

fective tale. Smith describes the spaceliner Arcturus being
sliced apart by rays from a mysterious spherical spaceship
while en route to Mars; the fragments are towed toward
Jupiter. By luck, one fragment contains scientist "Steve"
Stevens and beautiful, young Nadia Newton, daughter of the
director of the IPC (Inter-Planetary Corporation). The two
manage to steer their chunk of spaceship out of the debris
and land on Ganymede, where they fall in love, recharge the
power stores of their vessel, and begin constructing a
broadcasting device to contact Brandon and Westfall, Steve's
friends who also are the top human scientists. On a brief
cruise, Steve and Nadia encounter the humanoid natives of
Titan, also under attack by the spherical ships of the utterly inhuman and intractable Hexans from Jupiter.
(Meanwhile, the other survivors of the Arcturus have been
rescued by humanoid natives of Callisto, also the Hexans'
enemies.) With an assist from the friendly aliens, Steve
and Nadia signal Brandon and Westfall's ship, which rushes
to the rescue just in time to defeat a Hexan supership that
had been built to counter the human-aided Callistans.
Meanwhile, the Vorkuls, still another alien race--this one
from the South Pole of Jupiter, attack and apparently
destroy the Hexan stronghold at the North Pole. The humans
rescue one survivor in a disabled Vorkul spaceship, letting
him return home after treating his wounds. And so the survivors of the Arcturus complete their journey to Mars, over
a year late.

Smith obviously left the door open for more books in
the series. The Hexans, for one thing, have been defeated,
but they are so ferocious that they are dangerous as long as
any remain alive. The Vorkuls, meanwhile, are a fascinating
problem themselves--sympathetic on their own terms but alien
and difficult to work into human schemes. Not to mention
the natives of Callisto and Titan . . . . Yes, a lot could
be done with the situation at the end of Spacehounds. Even
so, the plotting of this novel is a good deal tighter than
Smith's earlier stories, and he gives a pleasing sense of
completeness to the work by focusing the opening chapter on
the IPC's efforts to maintain extreme accuracy in
navigation, time computation, etc., then concluding the
novel with the Arcturus' message to the Martian landing
field: "'IPV Arcturus; Breckenridge, Chief Pilot; trip number forty-three twenty-nine. Checking in--four hundred
forty-six days, fifteen hours, eleven minutes, thirty-eight
and seven-tenths seconds plus!'" (p. 257; p. 252), a finish
that neatly returns to the ordered setting shown in the
book's opening.

Characterization is also well handled. In particular,

for the first time since he wrote The Skylark of Space with Mrs. Garby's help, Smith tackles the opening stages of a love affair. To be sure, the love between Steve and Nadia is very much within the conventions of popular literature, but it is smoothly handled. Even its abruptness may be justified as showing the physical/mental admiration and sheer mutual dependence of the two young survivors. It also is true that their avoidance of sexual intimacy while they are marooned on Ganymede requires extreme willpower; they agonize verbally, but they manage to keep their hands off each other. To a certain extent, this simply reflects the mores of the time. In Smith's fiction generally, despite a real fascination with naked women (always presented as the cultural norm in an alien society and never described in detail, to be sure), passion is presented more verbally than physically: Look, but don't touch. Nevertheless, some practical considerations inherent in the situation do explain Steve and Nadia's restraint. Having confessed that they love and want each other, the two decide that they should delay sex as long as there is a chance of repairing their ship and leaving Ganymede. This is an important qualification. It later is discovered that several other survivors have not waited. In a more secure refuge on Europa, several human couples have fallen together. Women passengers have tended to marry ships' officers (suggesting not merely what stalwart types the IPC officers are, but how dependence fosters love, as mentioned above). The inevitable result of these marriages is babies (p. 199; pp. 1194-195), complicating the survivors' lives considerably and thus reaffirming the rightness of Steve and Nadia's decision. To modern readers, this may seem faulty extrapolation, since birth control devices have become so readily available now. Nevertheless, the behavior of the others shows the strength of the urge Steve and Nadia control. The whole situation can be contrasted to Vonnegut's Cat's Cradle, in which a clear-headed young woman prevents the despairing, purposeless narrator from copulation with her:

> she said to me, gently, "It would be very sad to have a little baby now. Don't you agree?"
> "Yes," I agreed murkily.
> "Well, that's the way little babies are made, in case you didn't know."(3)

Smith's characters do know, and the superior ones manage to control themselves as long as necessary not to be sad if a baby is made. The controlling of sexual drives is not so much a moral victory as it is a rational concentration on an important task. Steve and Nadia's success in their efforts, thus, is not a reward for virtue; it is the natural consequence of applying disciplined intelligence to a problem.

In fact, one of the clearest elements of Spacehounds of IPC is its basically relativistic viewpoint. That was part of Smith's writing from the start, as shown in the discussion of religion and clothing in The Skylark of Space; in Spacehounds of IPC, however, Smith uses aliens repeatedly to show how conditioned a race is by its norms, yet how important it is to grow past that conditioning. Early in the story, for example, Steve and Nadia discuss briefly a popular science-fiction romance of their time, to which Steve objects:

> "It's fundamentally unsound. Look at our nearest neighbors, who probably came from the same original stock we did. A Tellurian can admire, respect, or like a Venerian, yes. But for loving one--Pooie!" and he held his nose in a pantomine of disgust. "Beauty is purely relative, you know" (p. 101).

So are most things. Steve and Nadia repay their Titanian rescuers by going down to the surface of Saturn to repair a power plant that the fragile, super-cold, poison-breathing humanoids would have extreme difficulty doing by themselves; as Steve works,

> the Titanians clustered about their visiray screens, watching, in almost unbelieving amazement, the supernatural being who labored in that reeking inferno of heat and poisonous vapor--who labored almost naked and entirely unprotected, refreshing himself from time to time with drafts of molten water (p. 115).

All the strong adjectives of this passage, of course, show the Titanians' viewpoint. Its fundamental unsoundness--or at least relativity--is shown by the last word, which brings the reader back to the Tellurian perspective. The point is made again, in reverse, when the two Tellurians observe a Titanian foundery, described in (to readers) strictly normal terms:

> Men clad in asbestos armor were charging, tending, and tapping great electric furnaces and crucibles, shrinking back and turning their ar-

mored heads away as the hissing, smoking melt
crackled into the molds from their long-handled
ladles (p. 119).

Nadia is not impressed ("'Of course it's hot there--
foundaries are hot'"), until Steve reminds her "'That stuff
that they are melting and casting, and that is so hot, is
not metal but ice!'" (p. 119).
Throughout Spacehounds of IPC, Smith points out that
different cultures naturally produce distinctive attitudes
in their individual members, and that the attitudes may be
quite valid for each individual at a given time--but that
one must not imagine that his attitude is the only valid
one. In particular, one must not take the Hexan attitude of
instinctive, utter hostility to any different race or
culture. By controlling the readers' reaction, Smith uses
the Vorkuls to demonstrate this yet again. They first are
introduced in scenes "translated" and explained directly by
the omniscient author, who is free to describe two of the
monstrous-looking beings leaving an athletic contest, argu-
ing "quite like two Earthly experts after a good boxing
match" (p. 212). The human characters in the story encounter the Vorkuls without the advantage of verbal understanding and emotional empathy, and they don't know what to make
of the aliens. As Nadia comments when the wounded survivor
they have rescued departs without thanks,

> "Here we saved his life, and I fed him a lot of
> my candy, and we went to all the trouble of
> bringing their ship back here almost to Jupiter
> for them, and then they simply dashed off
> without a word of thanks or anything! . . . .
> Why, they don't think straight--as Norman would
> say it, they're full of little red ants! Why
> they aren't even human!" (p. 250)

As Smith's use of italics shows, Nadia is exaggerating the
case for human emotion. Brandon replies more reasonably:

> "Sure not . . . . They couldn't be, hardly,
> with their makeup. But is it absolutely neces-
> sary that all intelligent beings should possess
> such an emotion as gratitude? Such a being
> without it does seem funny to us, but I don't
> see that its lack necessarily implies anything
> particularly important" (p. 250).

Such a difficult understanding--the acquisition of calm

physical and emotional tolerance--is the reward for experience in Spacehounds of IPC.

Nadia's attitude is not as easy to simply dismiss as that, however. One place it appears again is the climax of Triplanetary, in which Clio almost paraphrases Nadia's words in her final, negative comment on the Nevians. For that matter, several things in Spacehounds of IPC are echoed in Triplanetary. The unemotional attitude of the Vorkuls foreshadows that of the Nevians (though their physical exuburance also foreshadows the Valentians, especially Worsel). The Triplanetary League is a union of Earth, Mars, and Venus, existing after an interplanetary war with the mysterious Adepts of North Polar Jupiter; in Spacehounds of IPC, the Corporation includes Earth, Mars, and Venus, and the Hexans' main stronghold is at the North Pole of Jupiter. I am not suggesting that Spacehounds is a direct prequel for the Lensmen novels. Smith worked very hard to create the universe of that saga as a thing by itself. Nevertheless, Spacehounds does reveal some of the materials out of which the Lensmen universe was created.

The Vortex Blaster originated as a series of short stories written for F. Orlin Tremaine's new magazine, Comet Stories. Actually, only the first story, "The Vortex Blaster," appeared in Comet (July 1941) before the magazine folded; the remaining two in the truncated series, "Storm Cloud on Deka" and "The Vortex Blaster Makes War," appeared in another short-lived magazine of the period (Astonishing Stories, June 1942 and October 1942). Then Smith returned to work on the Lensmen novels, of which the "Vortex Blaster" stories are an offshoot.

The novel based on these stories is understandably somewhat episodic. Essentially, it is the story of Neal "Storm" Cloud, whose family has been consumed by one of the uncontrollable atomic vortexes that burst out for no apparent reason in nuclear power plants. At the beginning, Cloud is suffering intensely--until he realizes that with his gift of instant mathematical calculation he could pinpoint the moment that a bomb could snuff out a vortex. With this purpose in life, he becomes the Vortex Blaster, and begins traveling from planet to planet. Along the way, he acquires a persistent enemy in Fairchild, who deliberately creates vortexes to hide evidence of his drug ring; a crew of basically humanoid aliens from different planets after he rescues them during an interplanetary war; and a cyberneticist and self-trained telepath, Joan Janowick, assigned to study Cloud so she can duplicate his abilities with a computer. Eventually, as Cloud's own mental powers expand

with Joan's stimulus, he discovers that the vortexes are in-
cubators for a race of energy beings; once he contacts them
and they put out the dangerous vortexes, the problem is
solved.

Actually, The Vortex Blaster is one of Smith's more interesting non-series books because it shows hints of how he
could have worked in another mode. Of all Smith's novels,
The Vortex Blaster comes closest to being what literary
critics would call a novel of character. It shows a person
who is complicated, pushed by a genuine drive toward pur-
poseful life and another drive toward easeful death. Smith
shows this anguish clearly but briefly; it soon is clear
that Cloud's drive to live is more urgent. Cloud consciously hopes to find an honorable death while extinguishing vortexes, but even when he runs into trouble on his
first mission, "with one arm and one leg and what few cells
of his brain were still in working order, he was still in
the fight. It did not even occur to him until long after-
ward that he was not going to make any effort whatever to
avoid death [his conscious intent prior to the event]" (p.
22). Smith presents this in understated, almost ironic
terms; Cloud is not aware of what is happening to him at the
time. Later, during another mission, he reflects when he
has no activity to occupy his thoughts:

> During such periods of inaction as this, he
> was wont to think flagellantly of Jo and the
> three kids [his family]; especially of Jo. Now,
> however, and much to his surprise and chagrin,
> the pictures which had been so vividly clear
> were beginning to fade. Unless he concentrated
> consciously, his thoughts strayed elsewhere: to
> the last meeting of the Society; to the new
> speculations as to the why and how of super-
> novae; to food; to bowling--maybe he's better
> start that again, to see if he couldn't make his
> hook roll smoothly into the one-two pocket in-
> stead of getting so many seven-ten splits (p.
> 49).

Instead of thinking of his dead family, Cloud gets up and
fixes supper. Smith does not stress this change. It is
treated as perfectly routine, but that is the point: it is
purely natural to grow out of grief, to put aside the
"flagellant" practice of savoring what is lost so one can
take care of physical needs, now.

The Vortex Blaster shows the natural stages of human
growth out of grief-shattered isolation into reintegration

with the world. It does so, again, without calling attention to the process, simply showing it in action; at each stage, Cloud does only what is natural, what he has prepared himself for by earlier growth. The passage just quoted above is prefaced by the statement that "Neal Cloud lived alone. Whenever he decently could, he traveled alone and worked alone. He was alone now . . ." (p. 49)—a perfectly natural condition for someone who sees himself as now and forever alone because of the death of his family. In the next episode, however, Cloud finds himself in the middle of an interplanetary war, and he is puzzled how to show the alien beings involved how foolish they are:

> These people [the aliens—another example of Smith's casual acceptance of merely physical difference] didn't stand the chance of a bug under a sledge-hammer, but they'd have to be killed before they'd believe it. A damned shame, too. The joy, the satisfaction, the real advancement possible only through cooperation with each other and the millions of races of Galactic Civilization—if there were only some means of making them believe . . . (p. 68).

As it happens, the aliens have been reading Cloud's mind. Consequently, they do believe. And because Cloud's thinking itself has clarified to the point that he can see and believe too, he is prepared to accept the gratitude and offer of loyal service from the people he has rescued. Thus, the The Vortex Blaster I acquires a crew and, thus, Cloud continues "the real advancement possible only through cooperation." In his telepathic contact with Joan, also, Cloud discovers he still has the capacity for intimate contact with another person, balanced with respect for the other's privacy. He discovers that it is not disloyalty to the dead to love the living.

As this happens inside the characters, the nominal plot shrivels. The extinguishing of vortexes becomes a perfunctory matter. Even the scheming of Fairchild is of secondary importance; the death of that nemesis is almost reduced to farce, as the cat-humanoid Vesta the Vegian plots the protracted torture of Fairchild after the latter has murdered her brother, then is disconcerted to find that she has killed him in her initial attack: "'His neck . . . it's . it's broken! From such a little, tiny pull as that? Why, anybody ought to have a stronger neck than that!'" (p. 170). Then she lays aside her grief and returns to the party she had been enjoying earlier. Vesta, too, has a good sense of what is natural. She knows how much energy should be spent on grief but also when to turn one's attention to finding joy and satisfaction in living.

In short, The Vortex Blaster shows Cloud's step-by-step clarification of his thinking while he prepares himself to do a useful task. At the novel's end, with the vortexes under control, Smith comments that "'Storm 'Cloud, Vortex Blaster, was out of a job" (p. 191). Actually it is quite clear the Cloud's real work has just begun—the human job of developing, growing, becoming a better representative of the best of what we call humanity.

Was Smith's concentration on character in The Vortex Blaster deliberate? It is impossible to be sure, but probably not. The story works wholeheartedly within the vein of science-fiction adventure perfected by Smith. In this case, however, Smith cannot follow his familiar technique of enlarging scope and scale; Cloud lives in the Lensmen's universe, and his activities would interfere with theirs if expanded too far. Thus, since the action cannot enlarge, Smith is led to expand the character instead. There also is a problem of form. Smith liked stories that continued, building steadily. When forced, by the too-infrequent publication of schedules of the magazines in which these stories were published, to write short fiction, he faced the problem of doing something satisfying within short episodes. Unable to develop action as he would have preferred, he managed to give the sense of a completed event in each story by showing Cloud learning a lesson each time, passing through a stage of development.

Thus, whether Smith undertook the stories that became The Vortex Blaster as a deliberate experiment in characterization or whether he was forced to concentrate on character, this novel does a rather deft job of something Smith almost never cared to tackle elsewhere. As such, it has a special place in his work.

The Galaxy Primes was published as a serial in Amazing Science-Fiction Stories (March-May 1959) and later as a paperback original by Ace Books (1965). Smith reportedly was upset at how the novel was edited for magazine publication, but the Ace book simply followed the magazine version.(4) Consequently, a reader should be wary of putting too much weight on a text that may not fully represent what Smith intended. Nevertheless, the novel is unusually interesting as the first novel Smith produced wholly afresh after finishing the Lensmen novels (and the associated The Vortex Blaster); it also is interesting as Smith's most deliberately "racey" novel.

73

The story of The Galaxy Primes is considerably looser than usual for Smith. Briefly, two male-female, super-esper pairs are thrown together in an experimental psi-powered starship. They make apparently random jumps from star to star, discovering many humanoid races who also are struggling to get psi powers under control. At the same time, there is considerable tension and jockeying for sexual-emotional position among the Tellurians. Finding how to control their ship, they start organizing the strongest espers from all planets into an organization that will encourage human development while preventing domination by any individual. While this is going on, the man and woman who have the strongest powers and who thus have been unable to imagine a stable relationship between themselves, discover they can live together after all.

Even this sketchy summary suggests the emphasis on interpersonal relationships that makes this such an atypical story for Smith. There probably were several reasons for this difference, the first being Smith's desire to write something different, "modern." In particular, the novel may be seen as an attempt to ride a then-current wave, the exploration of psionics championed by Astounding's John W. Campbell, Jr. Smith also, to judge from some pre-publication remarks in the fanzine Science-Fiction Times, may have believed that the stress on sex was what modern readers wanted.(5)

Besides this, The Galaxy Primes actually is the culmination of a constant subcurrent in Smith's works: nudity or semi-nudity, coupled with pantingly-verbalized sexual yearning. To some extent, Smith deliberately used nudity to point out the relativism of cultural values. To some extent, the expressions of desire are used to show the flesh-and-blood side of his sometimes-pristine heroes and heroines. Certainly Smith does not have the pornographer's obsession with oversized genitals attached to cipher-souled acrobats. Nevertheless, many of Smith's works show a delight in imagining unclothed bodies and a hovering fascination with what one could do if one would.

Most important, however, The Galaxy Primes is the logical and necessary outcome of the thorough exploration of the physical universe, taken to the limits of human imagination in the Lensmen novels. The exploration of character was the main challenge left to Smith. In his own way, before other writers announced their realization years later, Smith must have discovered that "Inner Space" was as intriguing a realm as outer space.

But the novel is much less than satisfactory, however one accounts for its bent. Focusing on the interrelationships of the characters, Smith left the exterior action very sketchy. There is little background for the bickering that fills the foreground. Unlike Smith's earlier novels, the narrative does not drive steadily from one event to another; the plot gives little feeling of urgency. The problems that do exist are talked about, kicked around in endless conversation, more than demonstrated.

This drifting, rambling tone is unfortunate, because Smith may really have something of importance to show. His characters' cantankerousness may be explainable as a preference for words rather than deeds, a fear of significant actions. They may be talking so much to avoid actions that would show their lack of ability to perform the most important action of joining with someone else at anything more than the most superficial level. Smith does a rather good, subtle job of showing his hero and heroine becoming aware of their need to marry, even while they are sneering at each other. He also is rather good at showing them sobered by the difference in perspective as they come to see all humanity as cells within a vast, inconceivable organism. But--again--the path to that insight is a pure intuitive leap, talked about rather than shown. There is no urgency about anything except the talk-sex-talk relationships of the characters.

In short, the novel is an honorable failure. Reading it is as disturbing as watching a man trying to get through a barrier in his path by beating it apart with his forehead.

Masters of Space was first published as a two-part serial in Worlds of IF Science Fiction (November 1961-January 1962), as a collaboration between Smith and E. E. Evans. Evans was one of Smith's long-time fans; First Lensman is dedicated to him, and his reading assistance is acknowledged at the end of Second Stage Lensmen. Moreover, Evans' own writing was deeply influenced by Smith; his first novel Man of Many Minds (Fantasy Press, 1953), for example, is an extrapolation in juvenile terms of the Lensmen's power to control the minds of nearby animals. It makes sense, thus, that Evans would very much want to collaborate with Smith--and that Smith would agree to complete the book that his dying friend was working on. I have heard various descriptions of what Smith was given to work with, ranging from a stack of sketchy notes to a finished manuscript with a few gaps left to be filled in. From the published version, it is impossible to guess which writer is responsible for which portions, and the novel may best be considered a work by Smith.

As such, Masters of Space continues the ruminations

about sex and intimacy that surfaced in The Galaxy Primes.
It also continues the fascination with the mental-physical
superman that is another continuing vein in Smith's work.
However, it deals with these issues in a rather perfunctory
manner. The story line is choppy, with little preparation
for events and little discussion of consequences. When, for
example, Tellurians realize that they must let their bodies
be physically transformed into super-durable alien material
to be able to acquire the knowledge left by their distant
ancestors, they express a few verbal hesitations but no real
doubt. And everyone chosen to become superhuman simply
leaps at the chance and seems eager to live sensuously ever
after. Thus, although the novel continues many of Smith's
themes and includes some fresh notions, it lacks the connected drive that makes Smith's other novels memorable. It
is by far the weakest book to carry his name.

The last book Smith prepared for publication was Subspace Explorers (New York: Canaveral, 1964). Essentially,
the first two chapters had appeared as a novelette in the
July Analog, but Campbell rejected Smith's sequel(s) to that
story.
Probably the whole story would have been too difficult
to follow through a series of magazine pieces. Even taken
as a novel, Subspace Explorers is a rather perplexing
performance. The plot is prohibitively dense to summarize.
In the first pages, acting on hunch, spaceman Carlyle Deston
approaches oil heiress Barbara Warner, discovers they both
are espers, and marries her immediately. Their spaceship is
wrecked in subspace; however, they, another couple (who turn
out to be espers, too), an elderly scientist (ditto), a
gangster and his cronies, and a malcontent spaceman survive.
After the bad guys are done away with before they can murder
the good guys, the survivors manage to drain the massive
energy their ship has picked up and get themselves rescued
about the time a child is born to each couple. All this,
remember, happens in the first two chapters. From there,
Smith races through the flight of far-thinking capitalists
from a union-strangled Earth; development of psionic
abilities on a large scale; attack by a company-dominated
planet; discovery and defeat of a Commie world, New Russia;
and several other subjects. The thing that gets the least
attention, in fact, is the exploration of subspace.
A natural first reaction of the novel is confusion; it
seems wildly over-condensed, with detailed scenes of domes-
tic banter interspersed with sweeping summaries or commen-
taries that change the direction of the action jarringly.
In particular, villains (such as the gangsters in the open-

ing chapters or the Nameless One, Dictator of West Hem, and his stooge, the West Hem Secretary of Labor) are set up and then obliterated without warning—and without impact on the reader. More seriously, conflicts of forces and ideas are set up and then raced past at bewildering speed. The space battles are rather perfunctory, for example, having nothing of the sweep and excitement of the battles in the Lensmen novels. Finally, the story feels as if the characters were lost in the abrupt changes of direction; regardless of "characterization," the people have little chance to state ideas and represent positions.

At the same time, Subspace Explorers can be defended. For one thing, the story obviously is broken off well before its conclusion. Treating the novel as if it were a complete work may be less than fair. Throughout Subspace Explorers, characters comment on the uncanny way coincidence operates in the action, and they suggest that some "operator" must be manipulating events. Then the action rushes along, and the concern is buried again. It seems likely, however, that Smith meant to do more with that idea, possibly tying it to the children of the subspace survivors, who gestated while the ship was charged with the mysterious energy of subspace. Also, the novel breaks off with an important issue pending: the capture of New Russia has brought the Free World psionicists in contact with Communist psionicists who are quite convinced of the ethical correctness of their viewpoint and thus extremely dangerous. At the end of the book, Smith simply sets up this problem, then literally and figuratively adjourns the meeting. In all, vital issues and plot elements are deliberately left dangling, to be picked up in a book that would continue the story.

The most attractive thing about Subspace Explorers, even its incomplete condition, is the energy with which Smith attacks his story. The fourth chapter, showing union troubles in an aluminum mine, is much more detailed than it needs to be for the plot, but it is lively and vigorous. Later, when Smith describes the Plastics' planet, World, his satire on company life as religion is again something of a digression, but it is a lively digression. Generally, whenever Upton Maynard, the dynamic leader of Galactic Metals, appears on the scene, Smith's evident approval brings the action to life.

What Smith manages to do, through Maynard, is resolve his detestation of big business, evident from The Skylark of Space on, versus his distrust of the mindless, gutless mass of humanity. In Subspace Explorers, Capitalism becomes the protector of individualism. In a kind of Darwinism, the fittest human beings have survived by escaping Earth; un-

77

willing to trade their freedom for security, they have gone into space, settling new planets and forming a kind of partnership--fair wages plus profit-based bonuses in return for loyal service--with their employers. The people who choose to stay on Earth or who choose to immigrate there from one of the colonized planets are described as "serfs," no matter what system of government they live under. Smith uses this natural inferiority to justify some ethically hazy tactics by the good guys' psionicists before an important election on Earth, and the question of what to <u>do</u> with the mess on Earth is another of the issues left unresolved at the novel's end. Nonetheless, Smith has managed to face up to some vital contradictions and work into, if not through, a resolution. Essentially, as readers of Smith's other works would expect, the novel justifies those who have too much energy and nerve to play it safe. They may face the possibility of failure, but they will risk everything they have, confident they can pull a dangerous enterprise together.

As such, even in its unfinished condition, <u>Subspace Explorers</u> may be a fitting conclusion to Smith's work, a not ignoble demonstration of what his vision as a science-fiction writer was all about.(7)

Short Fiction and Pastiches
        Smith's approach to writing kept him from writing many stories that could be confined to one volume, let alone a few pages. To fill the short story collection <u>The Best of E. E. "Doc" Smith</u>, the editors were forced to include excerpts from <u>The Skylark of Space</u> and <u>Triplanetary</u>, the separately-published stories that later became the opening chapters of <u>The Vortex Blaster</u> and <u>Subspace Explorers</u>, the chapter Smith wrote for a round-robin fanzine serial <u>Cosmos</u> (published separately as "Robot Nemesis" in 1939), and the three separate short pieces Smith ever had published. Even in these later cases, however, the stories obviously are only the beginnings of longer works. Smith simply was unable to continue them. Others did. Therefore, these works best can be discussed as the inspirations of continuing works by other writers, generally as part of the works showing Smith's direct influence.

        In the March 1953 issue of <u>Other Worlds Science Stories</u>, during one of his periodic demonstrations of what an exciting science-fiction editor he could be when he chose, Ray Palmer published "Tedric," aptly described as a "story of science and swashbuckling adventure." A sequel, "Lord Tedric," appeared in the March 1954 issue of Palmer's <u>Universe</u>. No more in the series were published, as Palmer's magazines expired or slid away into bargain-basement occultism.

Actually, the Tedric series is one of the most frustrating of Smith's incomplete works because it is such an uncommonly deft reworking of super-science and sword-and-sorcery adventure. Smith describes scientists of the far future trying to change the course of history to prevent the extinction of humanity that is imminent by their time. By traveling back in time and influencing the ironmaster Tedric, they can help his primitive state evolve into a dominant force in the world. The stories are interesting in two major ways. For one thing, Tedric is not just another Conan imitation, too dumb to think his way out of problems but too brawny to need to. Tedric is naive (and Smith manages some deft satire of religion in Tedric's deification of the scientist who advises him), but he is not stupid. Again, Smith is showing a character learning to use his mind; as King Phagon advises Tedric, "'You know not how to think . . . 'Tis a hard thing to learn; impossible for many; but learn it you must. . . .'"(8) By showing the stimulus that contributes to each stage of Tedric's growth, Smith is unusually successful at actually showing the character developing. Another interesting thing about the Tedric stories is the framework. As the scientist Skandos changes the past, his world of the future vanishes. He, Skandos One, must kill and replace the Skandos of each new future, still intervening in Tedric's career to drive history into the path he desires. This is a morally challenging, mind-stretching notion, and it would have been interesting to see how Smith could have brought it to a conclusion.

In 1978, 1979, and 1981, three novels by Gordon Eklund were published, blurbed as "a new series conceived by E. E. 'Doc' Smith." Lord Tedric, Space Pirates and Black Knight of the Iron Sphere have only a remote connection to Smith's stories. Eklund's Tedric is a man who somehow has been transported to another universe by the scientists of the planet Prime, to save humanity from a shadowy Evil lurking outside the decadent Empire of Man. Some of the names are the same (the Scientist who speaks to Tedric at the end of the first novel, for example, is called Skandos), and the Scientists vaguely echo the role of the Arisians in the Lensmen novels; nevertheless, the books show little of Smith's inventiveness. Eklund's Tedric is a more fallible, groping character than Smith's, but his apparent complexity is simply that of any hero in a modern paperback novel. The unfolding complexity of Eklund's plot is merely a deft reshuffling of conventional elements, not a transformation of them. Overall, Eklund's novels are smoothly written, sometimes witty, but fairly conventional and quite forgettable.

The last short piece Smith published was a novella, "Imperial Stars," in Worlds of IF (May 1964). This also was obviously the first part of a longer work, though it gives less sense of development than the Tedric series, more the feel of a straightforward espionage series, in which the main characters remain fundamentally unchanged from story to story as they move through different adventures. Even here, though, Smith does some interesting things with the characters and their situation.

Smith describes a future in which democracy has proved too ineffective to survive and so has been replaced on Earth by Communism. However, Communism has responded to human nature by developing a modified form of hereditary nobility and the profit motive, eventually becoming the heart of the Empire of Earth. Raised within this system, Smith's characters tie their sense of right and wrong directly to the survival of the Empire. The secret service of the Empire is loyal to the throne; if some villain succeeds in murdering his way to the throne, they will be loyal to him while he holds the throne. The characters justify this to themselves by insisting that the stability of the Empire would be threatened if anyone could freely challenge the system. What it amounts to is that might makes right. Smith certainly is fond of his central characters—members of the Family d'Alembert, aerialists from a high-gravity planet who can perform fantastic feats on lighter-gravity worlds—and he seems to endorse the rightness of their actions as top secret agents of the Empire. At least the people they fight are more murderous with less cause. He gets away with it primarily because he has a social setting that accounts for the characters' rather narrow outlook. The story may be seen as a typical product of the post-Fleming, pre-Watergate period, but it still abounds in possibilities for future stories.

The future stories in the Family d'Alembert series were written by Stephen Goldin, after Smith's death. The first, Imperial Stars, was published in 1976; it is an expansion and revision of Smith's story. It fleshes out and rationalizes the action that is thrown at the reader in the rather abrupt and choppy style of Smith's later writing, and it also adds some subplots and dilutes the dialogue's early-20th-century slang. Later books in the series are Strangler's Moon, The Clockwork Traitor, Getaway World, Appointment at Bloodstar, The Purity Plot, Planet of Treachery, Eclipsing Binaries, The Omicron Invasion, and Revolt of the Galaxy. They appear to be entirely Goldin's work, and they read like standard, well done, but quite conventional future-secret-agent tales. As of the most recent book, the series' plotline appears to have been completed.

Eklund's and Goldin's books are perfectly competent entertainment, in their own right, but they are safe and routine. Comparing them to the work of Smith, who was never content to be merely routine or comfortably safe, shows that despite the use of Smith's name these continuations of his story ideas are not worth much attention.

The Lensmen novels have inspired more interesting continuations. Shortly before he died, Smith gave William B. Ellern permission to write stories set in the Lensmen universe, after reading and approving Ellern's first such story, "Moon Prospector" (Analog, April 1966), a very capable tale of the defeat of a Boskonian intrigue on the Moon during the attack against the Galactic Patrol's Hill base as described in First Lensman. Ellern later wrote the novel New Lensman (serialized in Perry Rhodan #61-75, January-June 1975), showing what went on inside the Copernicus base while the events in "Moon Prospector" took place outside. The novel shows good use of the detailed scientific extrapolation and gadgeteering that Smith exploited so well, less effective plot construction in building incidents toward a climax, and little success in characterization (Smith's characters were vivid, whether complex or not). A novelette, "Triplanetary Agent" (Perry Rhodan #100-105, August-October 1976), also is set in the early days of the Galactic patrol, and Ellern indicates that he is working on additional stories showing the establishment of the Patrol and the exploits of the first Lensmen.(9)

Even more impressive is the attempt of David A. Kyle to add books to the Lensmen series. Kyle knew Smith and discussed unwritten stories with him. He does not, however, offer The Dragon Lensman (New York: Bantam, 1980), Lensman from Rigel (New York: Bantam, 1982), or Z-Lensman (New York: Bantam, 1983) as continuations of the series but as tales that fall in the gap between Second Stage Lensman and Children of the Lens. All manner of adventures could have happened in that time while the Kinnison children were being born and growing up. In the first novel, Kyle shows Worsel of Valentia encountering robot intelligences and the ghost of an Eich; in the second, Tregonsee of Rigel coordinates a web of intrigue and deception against the Spawn of Boskone; in the third, Nadreck of Palain VII is responsible for finishing off the limited-series' plotline. Kyle is very good at both working within the limits set by Smith's story and still introducing some new ideas of his own. The Boskonian robots are an intriguing concept, as are Arrow-20 (a machine that is developing intelligence on its own) and the Qu'orr "dreamers." In addition, Kyle does not hesitate to bend some of Smith's rules, introducing female characters in very responsible positions in all three novels. Overall, judging from Kyle's first novels, this is a group of books that will not feel out of place on the same shelf with Smith's.

NOTES

(1)   Edward Wood, "What A Time I've Been Reading," Science-Fiction Times, November 1965, p. 7.
(2)   In the chapter on Smith in Seekers of Tomorrow, Sam Moskowitz describes Smith's disappointment at having his next novel, Triplanetary, returned to him when Astounding Stories ceased publication, then being insultingly rejected by Wonder Stories, so that the novel eventually was published by Amazing after all.
(3)   (New York: Delta Books, n.d.), p. 215.
(4)   Noted by Al Lewis in his "Bibliography" for Ellik and Evans' The Universes of E. E. Smith, p. 256.
(5)   Bill Blackbeard, "New Doc Smith Novel 'Pure Sex & Psionics'--according to author," Science Fiction Times, First September 1958 issue, p. 3.
(6)   Seekers of Tomorrow.
(7)   First published in 1983, Subspace Encounter is a fascinating but perplexing addition to the story. Though blurbed as "The Sequel to Subspace Explorers," it appears actually to be Lloyd Arthur Eshbach's reconstruction of Smith's planned sequel, based on a partial manuscript, sections from Smith's first version of the immediate sequel to "Subspace Survivors," and Eshbach's own recollections of ideas Smith discussed with him. The book completes some, but not all, of the plot elements begun in Subspace Explorers, and it introduces new elements unconnected to the concerns developed in the first book. It contains some things that Smith did well and several that he never mastered. Until someone separates the different stages of composition/intention, this last novel to bear Smith's name remains a puzzle.
(8)   In Best of E. E. Doc Smith (London: Weidenfield & Nicholson, 1975), p. 172.
(9)   Phone conversation 8 August 1982.

VII

IMPACT AND ACHIEVEMENT

Many people will need no further reason to admire E. E.
"Doc" Smith's writing than his ability to tell a lively
story in vivid terms. "What more can you want?" they will
say. Others, uneasy about appreciating any fiction that
looks like wild escape literature, will ask "Why give so
much attention to a writer of primitive space opera?" In
fact, there are two reasons for looking seriously at Smith's
writing: the impact he had on science fiction and the
intrinsic merit of his own work.

Smith worked in the branch of science fiction labeled
space opera, usually noted for its stress on action and
startling ideas, without much attention to complex characterization or polished writing. Before Smith, space operas
by Edmond Hamilton and others had been simple transpositions
of adventure plots to space, the characters galloping from
galaxy to galaxy as they might have from castle to castle in
an historical adventure. Also before Smith, many non-
adventure science-fiction stories simply presented a mar-
velous discovery that the writer briefly scrutinized before
it was destroyed or otherwise lost. By his willingness to
keep thinking about new ideas, building further
extrapolations, following development after development,
Smith helped writers break free of their timidity; he also
stretched the formulas of space opera, finally transforming
that genre into something rich and strange in the Lensmen
novels.

After Smith, all science fiction bore the stamp of his
influence, most clearly in the writing of Jack Williamson
and John W. Campbell, Jr., but in many other writers' work
as well. And if they wrote other kinds of stories--as
Campbell did when he took the penname of Don A. Stuart for
restrained stories that hark back to the quiet pessimism of
early H. G. Wells--it was Smith's kind of story that they
were countering. That influence endures to the present. At
a panel during the 1982 World Science-Fiction Convention, a
group of writers including Larry Niven, Jack Chalker, Phyl-
lis Eisenstein, and Michael Resnick agreed that they stand
on the shoulders of earlier writers, in particular Doc Smith
because of his positive belief in the future as a place
where humans will be free to take significant action. Thus,
Smith's identification with the scientist, or rather with
the spirit of optimistic rationality that he attributes to

science, has become one of the foundations of science fiction.

Smith's influence shows up in unexpected ways, in unexpected places. Although his own work is apparently quite unlike Smith's, Irish writer James White remarks that it was Smith's stories that got him hooked on science fiction and relates his own Sector General medical science-fiction stories to the influence of Gray Lensman, in which he "discovered that there were aliens who were actually good guys, no matter how visually horrifying they might be."(1)

Obviously, we no longer are talking about purely historical influence. The most important reason to look seriously at Smith's writing is that his stories still live because they continue to transmit his concerns and interests to readers who may believe they are simply enjoying a lively story. Because Smith's humane, confident viewpoint shaped every story he wrote, readers feel the excitement of personal engagement even while they pick up unsuspected lessons in tolerance, patience, and willingness to attempt personal growth. At the same time, Smith reminds readers that they cannot depend on outside aid help and advice may come when needed, but essentially each person must look within himself for more intelligence and fortitude than he can imagine now.

As a writer, Smith sometimes was unable to get his message into words and human situations commensurate with his intent. He wrote within the limits of his time and of his talent. As do we all. Yet he played an important part in setting the direction of science-fiction's development, and he contributed to that development with honor and intelligence.

Or to put it another way:

From time to time, science fiction is described as a literary ghetto. It actually is more like a big-city ethnic neighborhood, sometimes suspicious sometimes expansive, uncertain exactly how it does relate to the larger community. People who explore the neighborhood can pick out the unique character of different streets and appreciate the personality of different edifices. They may notice one older structure in particular, an unassuming, hand-carpentered building with the name "Smith" worked into its wrought-iron fence. Before they hurry on to the chrome-and-plate-glass condos on the next block, they should pause and take a good look at the older home. It deserves attention. An honorable representative of the human spirit still dwells there.

NOTES

(1)   In "Interview: James White " conducted by Darrell
Schweitzer, <u>Science Fiction Review</u>, No. 43 (Summer
1982), p. 10.

VIII

SELECTIVELY ANNOTATED PRIMARY BIBLIOGRAPHY

"Atlantis." Actually Chapter II of Triplanetary, part of
the new material added to join the magazine serial to
the Lensmen series; published as a separate short
story in Journey to Infinity, ed. Martin Greenberg
(New York: Gnome, 1951).

Autobiographical Sketches. Thrilling Wonder Stories, June
1939; Other Worlds, March 1953.

The Best of E. E. 'Doc' Smith. London: Futura, 1975; rpt.
London: Weidenfield and Nicolson, 1976. The paper-
back edition precedes the hardcover. Introduction by
Philip Harbottle, Foreword by Walter Gillings. Con-
tents are "To the Far Reaches of Space" [excerpt from
The Skylark of Space], "Robot Nemesis," "Pirates of
Space" [excerpt from Triplanetary], "The Vortex
Blaster," "Tedric," "Lord Tedric," "Subspace
Survivors," and "The Imperial Stars." Also includes
"The Epic of Space" as Afterword.

"Catastrophe." Astounding Science Fiction, May 1938.
Smith's only published science-fact article. Since
the essay speculates on the creation of planets due to
the near collision of stars, it might be considered
background for the Lensmen novels; however, Smith
stresses how unlikely such an event is, suggesting
that our solar system (and the presence of life) may
be unique.

Children of the Lens. Astounding Science Fiction, November
1947-February 1948; Reading, PA: Fantasy Press, 1954;
rpt. New York: Pyramid, 1966.

"The Epic of Space" [essay]. In Of Worlds Beyond: The
Science of Science-Fiction Writing. Ed. L. A.
Eshbach. Reading, PA: Fantasy Press, 1947; rpt.
Chicago: Advent, 1964.

First Lensman. Reading, PA: Fantasy Press, 1950; rpt. New
York: Pyramid, 1964.

Galactic Patrol. Astounding Stories, September 1937-
February 1938. Reading, PA: Fantasy Press, 1950;
rpt. New York: Pyramid, 1964.

The Galaxy Primes. Amazing Stories, March-May 1959; New
York: Ace, 1965.

Gray Lensman. Astounding Science Fiction, October 1939-
January 1940; Reading, PA: Fantasy Press, 1951; rpt.
New York: Pyramid, 1965.

The History of Civilization. Title given the boxed, deluxe-
      binding set of the Lensmen novels. Reading, PA: Fan-
      tasy Press, 1955.
"The Imperial Stars." Worlds of IF Science Fiction, May
      1964. See also novel of the same name under
      "Pastiches."
"Introduction" to Man of Many Minds, by E. Everett Evans.
      Reading, PA: Fantasy Press, 1953; rpt. New York:
      Pyramid, 1959.
"Lord Tedric." Universe Science Fiction, March 1954.
Master of Space. Worlds of IF Science Fiction, November
      1961 and February 1962; London: Futura, 1976; rpt.
      New York: Jove/HPJ, 1979.
Masters of the Vortex. See The Vortex Blaster.
"Robot Nemesis." Thrilling Wonder Stories, June 1939.
      Separate publication of the chapter Smith contributed
      to the round-robin serial "Cosmos," originally pub-
      lished in the fanzine Fantasy Magazine, July 1934, un-
      der the title "What A Course!"
Second Stage Lensmen. Astounding Science Fiction, November
      1941-February 1942; Reading, PA: Fantasy Press, 1953;
      rpt. New York: Pyramid, 1965.
Skylark DuQuesne. Worlds of IF Science Fiction, June-
      October 1965; New York: Pyramid, 1966.
The Skylark of Space. Amazing Stories, August-October 1928;
      Providence, R.I.: Buffalo Book Co., 1946; rpt.,
      abridged New York: Pyramid, 1958. According to Al
      Lewis' bibliography in Ellik and Evans' book, the
      preferred hardcover edition is Providence, R.I.: Had-
      ley Publishing Co., 1947.
The Skylark of Valeron. Astounding Stories, August 1934-
      February 1935; Reading, PA: Fantasy Press, 1949; rpt.
      New York: Pyramid, 1963.
Skylark Three. Amazing Stories, August-October, 1930;
      Reading, PA: Fantasy Press, 1948; New York: Pyramid,
      1963.
Spacehounds of IPC. Amazing Stories, July-September 1931;
      Reading, PA: Fantasy Press, 1948; rpt. New York:
      Pyramid, 1963.
Spacehounds of IPC. Amazing Stories, July-September 1931;
      Reading, PA: Fantasy Press, 1947; rpt. New York:
      Ace, 1965.
"Storm Cloud on Deka." Astonishing Stories, June 1942. In-
      corporated in The Vortex Blaster.
Subspace Encounters. Edited and with an Introduction by
      Lloyd Arthur Eshback. New York: Berkley, 1983.
Subspace Explorers. New York: Canaveral Press, 1965; rpt.
      New York: Ace, n.d. Incorporates "Subspace

Survivors."

"Subspace Survivors." Astounding Science Fact & Fiction,
July 1960. Incorporated in Subspace Explorers.
"Tedric." Other Worlds Science Stories. March 1953.
Triplanetary. Amazing Stories, January-April 1934; Reading,
PA: Fantasy Press 1948; rpt. New York: Pyramid, 1965.
"The Vortex Blaster." Comet Stories, July 1941. Incor-
porated in The Vortex Blaster.
The Vortex Blaster. Hicksville, N.Y.: Gnome Press, 1960;
rpt. New York: Pyramid, 1968, under the title Masters
of the Vortex. A variant of the first edition exists
from Fantasy Press, same date, though the Gnome edi-
tion was printed first.
"The Vortex Blaster Makes War." Astonishing Stories, October 1942. Incorporated in The Vortex Blaster.
"What A Course!" See "Robot Nemesis."

Pastiches of Smith's Work

Eklund, Gordon. Black Knight of the Iron Sphere. New York:
Ace, 1981.
_____. Lord Tedric. New York: Baronet, 1978; rpt. New
York: Ace, 1978.
_____. Space Pirates. New York: Baronet, 1979; rpt.
New York: Ace, 1980.
Ellern, William B. "Moon Prospector." Analog Science
Fiction/Science Fact, April 1966. A novelette that
editor Campbell sent to Smith for his approval before
printing; in fact, Smith liked the story so much that
he gave Ellern written approval to write other stories
set in the Lensmen universe.
_____. New Lensman. Perry Rhodan [an odd magazine pub-
lished twice a month in the form of a paperback book]
#61-75, January-June 1975; London: Futura, 1976.
_____. "Triplanetary Agent." Perry Rhodan #100-105,
August-October 1976.
Garret, Randall. "Backstage Lensman," In Takeoff! Vir-
ginia Beach, VA: Donning, 1979. Actually a parody,
based chiefly on Gray Lensman. Garret reports that
Smith was amused by the piece and contributed some
touches of his own.
Goldin, Stephen. Appointment at Bloodstar. New York:
Jove/HBJ, 1978. Number five in the Family d'Alembert
series.
_____. The Clockwork Traitor. New York: Pyramid, 1977.
Number three in the Family d'Alembert series.
_____. Eclipsing Binaries. New York: Berkley, 1983.

Number eight in the Family d'Alembert series.
_____. Getaway World. New York: Pyramid, 1977. Number
four in the Family d'Alembert series.
_____. Imperial Stars. New York: Pyramid, 1976. Num-
ber one in the Family d'Alembert series. Based on a
short novel by Smith (see bibliography of Smith's
work), this is the only novel in the series that con-
tains any of Smith's writing.
_____. The Omicron Invasion. New York: Berkley, 1984.
Number nine in the Family d'Alembert series.
_____. Planet of Treachery. New York: Berkley, 1982.
Number seven in the Family d'Alembert series.
_____. The Purity Plot. New York: Berkley, 1980. Num-
ber six in the Family d'Alembert series.
_____. Revolt of the Galaxy. New York: Berkley, 1985.
Number ten in the Family d'Alembert series.
_____. Strangler's Moon. New York: Pyramid, 1976.
Number two in the Family d'Alembert series.
Kyle, David A. The Dragon Lensman. New York: Bantam, 1980.
_____. Lensman from Rigel. New York: Bantam, 1982.
_____. Z-Lensman. New York: Bantam, 1983.

IX

ANNOTATED SECONDARY BIBLIOGRAPHY

Items marked with an asterisk have not been personally examined; information on such material is drawn from Al Lewis' bibliography for the Ellik-Evans book.

Boggs, Redd. "Flight of the Skylarks." Spaceship [fanzine], #25 (June 1954), 2-12; rpt. in A Sense of FAPA, ed. Richard H. Eney (N.P.: Richard H. Eney, 1962), pp. 348-356. Admiring survey of the first three Skylark novels, using Smith's own comments on their writing. Discusses plotting and characterization, but finds deepest attraction of the books to be Smith's confidence in the perfectibility of mankind."

Clute, John. "E. E. Smith: 1890-1965." In Science Fiction Writers: Critical Studies of the Major Authors from the Early Nineteenth Century to the Present Day. Ed. E. F. Bleiler. New York: Scribners, 1982, pp. 125-130. Discussion of Smith's career and works that fails to credit him with most of the virtues this book has discussed, but that does praise him for doing very well at exuberant space operas of great scope. On its own terms, a carefully written and fair-minded appraisal.

E. E. "Doc" Smith: Father of Star Wars. West Warwick, R.I.: Necronomicon Press, 1977. Actually an interview conducted by Thomas Sheridan and titled "Galactic Roamer") first published in the fanzine Fantasy Review in 1948. Discussion of writing career, with brief survey of life and writing practices.

Ellik, Ron, and Bill Evans. The Universes of E. E. Smith. Chicago: Advent, 1966. Concordances to the Lensmen an Skylark series, along with the bibliographical information (by Al Lewis) and a sliver of critical commentary.

Eshbach, Lloyd Arthur. Over My Shoulder: Reflections On a Science Fiction Era. Philadelphia: Oswald Train, 1983. Personal and professional experiences with Smith by the founder of Fantasy Press.

Goldin, Stephen, interviewed by Kathleen Sky. An Hour With Stephen Goldin: "The Making of a Science Fiction Writer." Garden Grove, CA: Hourglass Productions, 1979. Taped interview, with considerable commentary on experience of working with Smith's writing and ideas in continuing the Family d'Alembert series.

Heinlein, Robert A. "Larger Than Life: A Memoir in Tribute to Dr. Edward E. Smith," In Expanded Universe: The New Worlds of Robert A. Heinlein. New York: Grosset, 1980; rpt. New York: Ace, 1981. Vigorous defense of the most often criticized aspects of Smith's writing (dialogue, plotting, relation of sexes, etc.) combined with praise of Smith as a person.

Lupoff, Richard. "Smith, E(dward) E(lmer)" in Twentieth Century Science-Fiction Writers, Ed. Curtis C. Smith. New York: St. Martins, 1981, pp. 507-508. Credits Smith with originating space opera; also defines material from which space opera was created and discusses Smith's influence on its development. Calls Smith an impressive "primitive" novelist in sense of vividness rather than subtlety of characterization, dynamism rather than polish of style, power rather than complexity of plot, and directness rather than ambiguity of theme."

*Moskowitz, Sam. "Doughnut Specialist Smith Blasts Vortices in His Spare Time." Astonishing Stories, June 1942.

_____. "E. E. Smith, Ph.D." In Seekers of Tomorrow: Masters of Modern Science Fiction. Cleveland: World, 1966, pp. 9-26; rpt. New York: Ballantine, 1967, pp. 17-33. Chapter on Smith is slight revision of "The Saga of Skylark Smith," Amazing, April 1964. Rich in details of Smith's professional life and writing career.

*Noda, Koichiro. "E. E. Smith and the Lensman Series." Sogen Suiri Koonaa, May 1966, Sogan Mysteries Corner, Special SF Issue #2.

*_____. "Kimball Kinnison--Lensman." SF Magazine (Hayakawa Pub. Co., Tokyo), March 1964. "Hero's Who's Who in SF Worlds #6."

*_____. "Richard Seaton." SF Magazine (Hayakawa Pub. Co., Tokyo), December 1963., "Hero's Who's Who in SF Worlds #4."

Pohl, Frederik. "Edward E. Smith, Ph.D." Worlds of IF Science Fiction, December 1965, pp. 4, 6. Obituary tribute, summing up Smith's accomplishments and influence.

Rogers, Alva. A Requiem for Astonishing. Chicago: Advent, 1964. Discussion-summary of Smith's works in context of their magazine publication. Pages 152-153 quote a letter describing Smith's planning and writing of the Lensmen novels.

Science Fiction Times [fanzine], November 1965. This issue

of the long-running newszine is devoted entirely to a memorial to Smith, with (sometimes brief) tributes by editor James V. Taurasi, Sr., Hugo Gernsback, W. R. Cole, L. Sprague de Camp, Joseph Ross, Robert Silverberg, Larry T. Shaw, Jay Kay Klein, Edward Wood, and P. Schuyler Miller. A brief checklist of Smith's writings by Ronald R. Eberle.

Stableford, Brian. "The Lensman Series," in Science Fiction Literature, Volume Three, ed. Frank N. Magill. Englewood Cliffs, NJ: Salem, 1979, 1183-1187; rpt. in Science Fiction: Alien Encounter, ed. Frank N. Magill. Pasadena, CA: Salem, 1981. Dismisses work as juvenile power fantasy that "probably allows the harmless exorcism of brutal impulses and the safe indulgence of antisocial sentiments."

_____. "The Skylark Series," In Survey of Science Fiction Literature, Volume Five, ed. Frank N. Magill. Englewood Cliffs, NJ: Salem, 1979, pp. 2091-2095; rpt. in Science Fiction: Alien Encounter, ed. Frank N. Magill. Pasadena, CA: Salem, 1981. Admits historical importance but believes modern readers can find no pleasure here.

*Van Riper, Anthony L. "Skylark Smith: An Appreciation." Dynamic Science Fiction, October 1953.

Weedman, Jane B. "E. E. Smith" in Twentieth Century American Science-Fiction Writers, Part 2: M-Z (Dictionary of Literary Biography, Vol. 8), ed. David Cowart and Thomas L. Wymer. Detroit: Gale, 1981, pp. 132-136. Survey of Smith's work that gives him credit as a pioneer in development of science fiction. Several bizarre judgments, such as statement that after The Skylark of Space, Smith "produced no other quality work until Skylark DuQuesne."